No Holds Barred

By

Peter R. Wicks

Poetry from the working-class view
of the life and times of an octogenarian old man

Grosvenor House
Publishing Limited

The right of Peter R. Wicks to be identified as the author of this
work has been asserted in accordance with Section 78
of the Copyright, Designs and Patents Act 1988

The book cover picture is copyright to Inmagine Corp LLC

This book is published by
Grosvenor House Publishing Ltd
Link House
140 The Broadway, Tolworth, Surrey, KT6 7HT.
www.grosvenorhousepublishing.co.uk

This book is a work of fiction. Any resemblance to
people or events, past or present, is purely coincidental.

A CIP record for this book
is available from the British Library

ISBN 978-1-78623-404-9

Foreword and Dedication

I was born in 1937 in a part of London adjacent to Hanover Square in South Kensington.

In my journey down life's highway my history has covered World War 2 and all other wars since then. These experiences have left an indelible mark on my memory bank and turned me into a very cynical person on all things human, especially where politicians and establishment figures are concerned.

Many of my poems are of a radical nature and express my dislike of those who exploit the poor and the underclass of this world, which has resulted in me becoming an atheist and a republican in my outlook as regards the future of Britain.

I wish to dedicate this book to my late wife, Sylvia, whom I loved dearly in the fifty-four years we were married. She displayed an extraordinary level of fighting instinct throughout her life and times.

I would like to thank my Facebook friends who badgered me to publish this book.

I hope that my poems give the reader an insight into my world, make them smile at my radical expressions and help people to remember the past and the present and how actions taken by individuals and the nation have affected us all.

Within this poetry the reader will see colloquial expressions used and the occasional swear word that limits itself to the F and B words, along with a few cockney expressions.

The Author

A Daughter is a Daughter

You have a child
In your early years.
With your eyes
Wide open
You fail to see
Your children grow
Up into maturity.

A daughter is yours
For all of your life
Even after marriage
As a young man's wife

But a son is a son
In his formative years,
A legacy for you of
Heartbreak and tears.

He marries one day
The girl of his dreams
But the girl that he weds
Is not all that she seems.

Possessive and jealous
Of his own mum and dad,
Of the love that they gave
When he was a lad.

So that adage is true
Of the wise men of old:
'A daughter
Is a daughter

For all of her life.
A son is a son
Till he takes a wife.'

A Day of Shame

Republican sickness is a shameful trait of an American party that preaches hate,

A greedy sickness of the monetary kind that rules out kindness. To the lower-class ones, as Republicans say, they can 'kiss our bums'.

Not a single Republican backed the bill that would give millions free care in hospitals and expensive Pills.

Something is lacking in the land of the free, as two-faced Americans, the well-off lot, divide up this Nation to the haves and have nots.

Their fellow Americans who are born for the gun, who lay down their lives for these Republican ones – Cannon fodder, a beast to beat who can die for the flag but never get sick.

Good for Obama. He stuck by his guns and dished out health care for all of its sons, that included the Poor and the downtrodden ones.

Power to the people.

A Letter to Mama

Mama, the killing
Won't stop.
My gun has seen
Children scream
When bullets
Mow them down mercilessly.

Mama, I can't take it
Anymore.
My shattered mind
Is in a turmoil.

Mama, when will
This killing end?
The things I'm doing
I can't defend.

Mama, humanity's
Gone mad
In this far-off place
Of desert sands.

Friends are dying
As this letter I write.
Tell them all at home
Of our horrible plight.

Please, Mama,
Make them see
How we kill needlessly
Just for oil
And mankind's
Evil, selfish greed.

A Pox on You All

A pox on the drug barons,
And on their greed and wealth,
For their denial of medicines
For the Third World's health.

A pox on the shareholders
Who sanction this greed,
Who turn a blind eye
To the dying in need.

A pox on all governments
With hands in the till.
Death is their medicine
For the Third World's ills.

A pox on you all,
Your humanity's in need.
You sanction this obscenity
In the name of pure GREED.

A Scream in the Night

Heed the child who
Screams in the night
And see that child
Who cringes in fright.

See their bodies
All battered and bruised,
This pitiful child
So badly abused.

Look at their faces
Distorted in pain
Through the anguish and
Terrible lone suffering
That's their parents' shame.

Look at the marks
So grisly and grim
On the body of the child
So frail and thin.

Look at the weapons
These parents will use
To batter young children
So badly abused.

They kick in their ribs
And break up their limbs
But no one hears
Their terrible SCREAMS.

Give them no pity
For the deeds that they do.
Think of that child
All battered and bruised.

For whatever the cause
Of the child beaters' plight,
For your god's sake get help
For the poor little mites.
Don't be an ostrich
And bury your head.
It could be too late
That child could be DEAD.

A Short History Lesson
of Times Past and Present
(For All You Tories Wearing Red Ties)

After the Second World War
The men of Britain were adamant
That they would not go back
To the status of the slave and master
Attitude of the pre-war days.
They had just fought a war
With blood and sweat not
To have the chains of servitude
Manacled to their bodies
When they returned home.

The war left Britain destitute
Without any help from the Marshall Plan
That created the new Europe –
For we in Britain were absolutely broke
And the Yanks offered no help whatsoever.

So after the war, this country
Kicked Churchill out of power
And it elected the Labour Party
With the biggest landslide victory of all times
And we had the one and only real socialist
Government this country had ever seen.

What happened then MUST happen again.
The Labour Party set about rebuilding
Our country by a wonderful means
Called NATIONALISATION.

Every industry that was in private hands
Was taken by the state for the good of
The many and not the few.
This included coal, electric, gas,
Water, shipping, trains, oil,
Post office, telephones, buses, trams,
Airports, airlines and great swathes
Of private lands. If it could benefit the people
It was nationalised.

Labour took from the rich and gave to the poor,
A Robin Hood of the 1940s.
We had our first National Health Service
And a free dental service,
Plus free prescriptions for all.

But then the Maggot came along
From the Tory Party whose first vile job
Was to stop the free school milk kids
Were getting and this earned her
The rightful name of Thatcher the Snatcher.

But Labour was getting soft
And had lost its balls. It elected a
Welsh windbag called Kinnock as its leader
Who set about to destroy
Labour's socialist ideology.
In later years he received a seat
In the House of Lords
For this bit of treachery.

So the Tory Party gained power
With a landslide election
With the Maggot as its leader.
She was more right-wing
Than Attila the Hun
But far deadlier.

She wanted to decimate
All that our brave men had
Fought and died for
In the Second World War –
'A country fit for heroes'.
And by all the unholy deeds
In this world, she did.

She set about to thieve and sell
The 'family silver' as Ted Heath
Once called it. Bit by bit she sold
It to her filthy rich friends in the City
And in her own party until all that was left
Was our NHS, but that was a sell-off too far.

Her own party chucked her out of office
When she caused mass riots
Over her hated poll tax bill
But all was not lost for the Tory Party.
A new face appeared on the catwalk
Of politics as Tory Blair...
This chap pretended to be a socialist
And a friend of the workers
And with the help of Ginger Kinnock
Became the new leader of the Labour Party.
Kinnock did away with Clause Four and
That bit of treachery signalled the end of
Socialism as my generation knew it

Tory Blair was the biggest disaste
To come the workers' way.
He spun his lies so much that he nearly
Went into orbit with his blatant untruths
About weapons of mass destruction crap
But it caused the death of countless people
In the conflict on desert sands.

Tory Blair continued to flog off Britain
But dressed in the sick little name of PFI.
This gave giant building firms like French Kier
The go-ahead to build hospitals for the NHS
Then charge the British public BILLIONS
In rent for the next thirty years.
Sick is not the word I use…

So Labour is a sham. It ditched its roots
Long ago to the gods of greed and corruption
And it will be obliterated at the next
Election and allow the hordes of
Nationalists or Ukip candidates
To gain seats in the halls of Westminster.

Well done, you greedy, selfish gits, well done,
For now the true spirit of the old left wing
Of the labour movement should rise from the ashes
Of the shell of the party that once represented
All the underdogs of this divided land.

A Spoke in the Wheel of Life

You're just a spoke in
The wheel of life,
Fixed to the middle
And to the rim

As round and round
We humans spin.

Where we go
And where we have been,
What we do
And what we have seen,

All will be revealed
When it stops its spin.

A Ticking Generic Time Bomb

Think of the kids.

Do you remember days of old
When courting your girl
Was the way it was done?
'Nookie' was the forbidden one.

But now it's one drink and off to bed.
Give me the days of the faithful wife.
We respected the one we would wed
When marriage was for all of your life.

Lust is now the name of the game –
Love vanished as old-fashioned ways.
Single mums with a string of kids,
Unknown fathers on one-night stands,
'Up the duff' for a council house,
A 'bun in the oven' and it's done.
Get your perks from
We tax-paying bums.

But a time bomb is ticking away
As these kids grow up to bonk one day.
Was that my cousin I shagged last night?
Or my uncle's brother or my mother's dad?
The biggest cock-up this world has seen
As inbreeding becomes so firkin rife.
You don't know who your dad is
Or that tart was not his wife.

So future kids that come this way
Must be tested for their DNA
Or the world of defective children
Is here to stay.

A Time to Think

Sitting in your favourite chair
Deep in thought with hypnotic stare,
This time is yours, a time to think
Of times gone by, of joy and grief.

The things you did, or didn't do,
Of ones you loved, who loved you too.
Stupid things you might have said
To friends and family, now long dead.

Wishing thoughts of bygone days
You wish and wish you could change.
Jumbled thoughts flash through your mind,
Death, corruption, all humankind.

You wish there were a magic pill
Taken by humans to cure their ills.
'Tea or coffee?', your loved one says,
As you wake with a start
From your thinking daze.

We have all been there.

A Tiny Link

A tiny link –
This minute thread
Passing on through
The family tree –
The DNA of insanity,
A corrupted gene.
So much heartache
This little gene brings.
Love is shattered
And dreams recede,
Hatred and violence
Now proceed.

Used and abused
As a battering ram,
Reviled and spat at,
Cursed and goaded
Every violent day
When this gene
Comes out to play.

Pleas for help
Fall on deaf ears
As this foul little gene
Brings rivers of tears.
Not a soul is listening
To the sorrowful plea,
'Is there anyone out there
Who will show me mercy?'

All Quiet On the Truthful Front

So the war is nearly won.
The last of our boys are
Are on the homeward run.

Now we want to know the truth,
The reasons why so many had to die
And WMD was such a pack of lies.

An in-depth inquiry of what went on,
Just the least we owe the mothers' dead sons.
An open court is so justified,
WE want to hear their pack of lies.

But the cowards can't face the cold dark truth.
Bush and Blair, both true Satan's sons,
Want truth's door SHUT on everyone.

So behind closed doors they spin more lies
Just like the bullshit they utter as truth.
The reason for war, the maimed and the dead,
The oil in the desert under hot Arab suns
Is the real bloody reason. They lied to everyone.

So wee Mr Brown will come crashing down
With the New Labour ship – the final disgrace
When he lies to the Nation, to the mothers' dead sons
And the whole of the world turns its back on this bum.

Change your mind, wee Gordie, change your mind.

Always and Ever

Was always and ever within my dreams
A lifetime of loving the simple things
Anyway – but always you're in my heart.
Always and ever, it was from the start
A dream we lived, so very long ago.
We vowed and declared our love would be
True and in this twilight of our times and the
Dreams of us two, I can still say, I love you,
My darling. I hope you do too.

Always 'I' and Never 'We'

The underbelly
Or the underclass,
The forgotten blacks
Of the working class,
African Americans.

The downtrodden ones
Who died in thousands
In the land of the free
As hurricane Katrina
Destroyed Mississippi.

Their screams for help
Fell on deaf ears
As the waters of death
Washed out their tears.

But if you were white,
Regardless of class,
Your overriding thought
Was to save your arse.
Helping others
Is alien to you.
It's always 'I' and never 'We'.
The shameful things
They didn't do
As death and carnage
Daily grew.

Just shut your eyes,
This horror will pass
But the memory of this
Will last and last
When African Americans
Start kicking
WHITE ARSE.

It's An Insular World

It's an insular world.
The elite must keep
A system of government
By establishment freaks.
Their rule is total.
They make the law
For us fools to keep
But rules are different
For the ruling elite.
It's another world
In Parliament Square,
Solicitors and barristers,
The great and the good
Stand there in Parliament
Where Oliver once stood.
Do as we say, not as we do:
A message from Parliament
Passed down to you.
The spirit of Cromwell
Jumps from his grave
To FREE his beloved people
These cretins enslaved.
He cuts off the fingers
With his ghostly sword
Of MPs and ministers
With hands in the pie
Who steal vast fortunes
Belonging to you and me.
'It must be this way,'

You can hear them cry,
As Oliver goes on cutting
Greasy, thieving fingers
From the nation's pie.

Armstrong and Aldrin

Armstrong and Aldrin
Were having tea
As Hollywood filmed
This hoax in the sixties.

The *Space Odyssey*
Of '68
Proved that
The moon walk
Was a fake.

The flag did flutter
In a wind?
But the moon
Is airless.
No breeze
Had ever been there.
But then again,
It could be true
Depending on
Your point of
View!

Backstabbing Chums

The knives are out
for Gordon Brown
As the Blairite women
Are after his crown.

These sick sisters,
Ex-Tony's babes,
'Tis an urgent request
That their CLPs
Chuck them out.

Old Labour
Is a bygone day
Of Tony Benn
But his socialist
Dream is not for them.

Their attitude to Labour
They can never defend.
PFI and private health
Goes hand in hand
With other MPs' perks.

They take this nation
As stupid fools
But we as the voters
Can see the writing
On the constituency walls.

Radical change,
A lurch to the left,
Take it all back
That once was all ours
So not one utility
Is a sacred cow.

Re-nationalise
The whole ruddy lot.
Clem and Nye!
Has Labour forgotten?

Your days are numbered
Blair's mouthy ones.
For the people of Britain
Can't stand
His backstabbing chums.

Beans on Toast

As I sit here eating my beans on toast,
I contemplate my world and times.
The darkness of my world is all-engulfing
With no light at the end of this long tunnel.
A world without end, someone once said.
'Rubbish,' I reply, for I see just a glimmer

But not a glimmer of hope for humankind
For this creature is long past his sell-by date.
Nature has plans afoot to end his disastrous reign.
Slowly but surely homo sapiens will vanish from Earth.

The seas will rise as the ice caps melt into fresh water
Thus diluting the lifeblood of all of Earth's salty seas.
Life in the seven oceans will all but disappear forever.

Global warming will accelerate, for our seven oceans
Played an important part in recycling carbon dioxide
But that's all by the by, as I demolish the last bean.
My plate is clean and I settle down to re-read
The Ragged-Trousered Philanthropists once more
To make sense of my life and times on Earth.

For Robert Noonan (Tressell).

Bedsit Prison

Four square walls, damp in spots,
Dirty curtains, brown with age,
Sash cord broken, missing pane
Letting in the cold wet rain.

Wallpaper peeling at the edge,
Patterns faded to greeny-red,
Flaking ceiling way up high
Cobweb-covered like snowflake
Sky.

Chipped enamel, rusted door, on
Two-ringed cooker caked in grease
For beans on toast, a night-time
Feast.

Iron bed with squeaking springs
Gives sleepless night and nightmare
Dreams.

Alone at night by the gas fire's glow
The ticking clock you well know,
Soft at first with its rhythmic beat,
Deafening later when you try to sleep.

A hole in the wall, where the floorboards
Meet, live the mice we hermits keep.
They roam the room late at night.
As sitting tenants, they're alright.

Bedsit prison, I know you well
With your battered furniture and
Musty smells. A single room
Or double share, we live our life
In this place called HELL.

Big Brother 1984?

Our freedoms are going, one by one.
We are clueless of what's going on.
A supergrass down every street,
Friends and neighbours dare not speak.

Surveillance cameras in every road,
Our civil liberties they erode.
You dare not think or talk aloud
When the thought police are around.

'They' want your genes, your DNA,
On the biggest computer of the day.
'They' want the profile of everyone
To point a finger or a gun!

There's a satellite camera in the sky
Tracking our movements until we die.
Those George Orwell days of '84
Are fact not fiction anymore.
Wake up, my friends, before it's too late,
Before we become the Big Brother state.

Bittersweet Chocolate

African kids as young as eight
Work ten hours without a break. They
Climb the trees for cocoa beans that create
The billions in far-off lands by child labour
That should be banned.

Your Easter eggs come from the sweat and tears
Of children who should be at school but are used
As slaves in tropical heat to cut down
Beans for chocolate bars for us to eat.

Bitter and sweet each bite we take of
Nestlé and Cadbury, the chocolate bunch
Who make their millions from every crunch.

Boycott it all this slave-made choc.
Leave it on the shelves and let
It rot. Say, 'Stuff you, and your disgusting
Morality', and tell all your shareholders
To climb the fucking cocoa trees.

Bluebottle Buzz

Our bins are dirty
And smelling quite rank.
We've made our protest
But on deaf ears it sank.

Bluebottles are buzzing
And the maggots do breed.
Complaining to a council
Will never succeed.

So post them a letter
With a maggot inside.
Write in the letter
For the cretins to see,

'Here is your maggot,
YOU recycle it for me.'

Get rid of this maggot
That is creating this stink
Before dumping you
As rubbish at the elections
WE speak.

Then bluebottles
Will buzz around
The jobs that you keep.

Blueprint of Life

Nature is blowing
In a vengeful wrath.
No human can stop
Its winds of change

As the fury of nature
Is becoming enraged.
The day is fast dawning
When nature will say,

Enough is enough
Of your stupid ways.
We gave you your
Chance on planet Earth,

This precious lone gem
In the Universe.
You've forfeited all rights
As the intelligent ones.
Now nature is angry
At what humans have done.

Your god is nature,
The giver of life.
It's deaf to religion
Or other controlling vice.

The blueprint of life
Is going to change
As nature all-powerful

Will surely arrange –
Wiping out all humans
Who destroy and deceive,
What nature created
For all living things.

Bodmin Moor

'Tis a tale of truths
That are laid within
A part of Cornwall,
The strange Bodmin.

A brooding place
With legends untold
Of ghosts and beasts
Haunting the visitor,
The strong and bold.
Stories I tell you
About to unfold.

The legends of Cornwall
Of the far distant past,
Giants and piskies
And Bolster
With the six-mile stride
Who drowned in his blood
In the bottomless pit,
Betrayed by his lover
Who pushed old Bolster
Into that pit.

But Jan Tregeagle
Of Bodmin Moor
Is the spirit most seen
Being chased at night
By the devil and hounds,
A blood-curdling sight.

Crooked Tregeagle
Stole from the poor,
Cheating his master
The Lord of Lanhydrock
Who punished poor Jan
To run with the hounds,
Chased by the devil
Over Bodmin's
Vast grounds.

So do not venture
Alone at night
For Bodmin Moor
Is haunted by knockers
And spriggans,
The ugly ones
Who feast on visitors
When night-time's begun.

Bonking Nuts

Travelled this road, more than three
Score years and ten, but the
Changes I've seen I would be
Stretched to describe them.

From war and a peace that I have
Never seen on planet Earth amongst
Human beings.

Technology and science march on the
Future's road but forgetting the millions
Who on the waste pits are thrown,
To fend for themselves,
To die on their own.

But the most disturbing trait that
This poet has seen is the changes in
Women since the PILL was conceived.

Gone is the gentle and fair kind of sex,
Gone is the housewife who brought up her kids
And gone are the families with one common name,
And in come the strangers to tempt and deceive
The gullible woman with sex for their needs.

But generations have grown up not knowing a dad.
They clear off and leave them once the pleasure
they've had.

Then the cycle of mothers who stand all alone,
with kids in the prams, with four more at home.
But these are the kids who have just left a school
Who never got guidance from mothers who are fools.

So women have changed and not for the best
And some are even growing man's hair on the chests.
They cuss and they drink and do everything we do
But marriage is dead and love's with it too.

We want it now, the pie in the sky.
We want any rich guy,
The old ones are best; we can screw
off his nuts till the old fart is dead,
No chance of babies, the pill is our pal.
We screw and we screw everything we can and
forget all our children and our stupid old man.
He can look after our kids like our parents
of old whilst we screw off our arse
And make the men pay for the burdens
they gave our mothers in old-fashioned days.

Long live the pill and a pox on love,
Long live lust and dirty old rich men (I'm free).

This old poet married in 1961 and we are still in love.
Marry for money and you spend the rest
Of your life looking for love.

Brainwashed

How we are brainwashed from birth to our death,
from religion at first at hellfire's behest.
Damnation to follow if you never obeyed
the words of some scriptures to the very last page.

The newspaper of sorts with a message to tout,
Vote for this, let all of you shout but the owner is
Using his media for him to brainwash you to vote
To do as he wishes and vote for some evil,
Some power con trick, to make his empire that
Richer with brainwashing tricks.

Look at your TV – now America is best, with
Hundreds of stations that pick at your minds and
Brainwash the States from the land to the sea,
With falsehoods of terror to stab at your brain
To make out your president is a Satan, again and again.

YouTube is crass, that couldn't care less as it
Stirs up the people with far-right creepiness. It
Fosters the liars, the hate and the shit that Hitler
Would be proud of and Joseph Goebbels would agree,
'Great propaganda for a fascist country.'

But America is wise and can see through this tripe,
The evil of Republicans on the extreme far-off right.
Greed is their Bible for making them rich,
With doctors and dentists and drug firms galore
Who won't open their wallets to the
destitute and the poor.

So ride a chariot of burning fire into the realms
Of these deniers. Burn out the wickedness in
Your midst. Get rid of brainwashers, the greedy ones,
And let America unite for EVERYONE.

Bread and Dripping

We kids were a hardy lot
Living on cabbage and spuds,
Hardships of war years I've not forgot.

Breakfast was a bowl of oats
Made with water, looking like glue.
You could swallow it down, after a chew.

But bread and dripping, my favourite bite
Better than Bovril or even black Marmite.
We spread the lot on bread, in those distant days,
Even condensed milk was all the rage.

Bread and dripping, from a Sunday roast,
Spread on bread, but best on toast.
A pinch of salt, it was done –
Taste the flavours till the very last crumb.

Even now, at 77, I remember margarine
Smeared on hair, but we drew the line
If mum used the dripping pot
For this was the best breakfast
We ever got.

Brigadoon

Deep within the highland mist
The echoes of a magical tune
A Scottish lilt called 'Brigadoon'.

Once a century it calls your name,
The village from the mystic past,
Enchantment blessed, heaven-sent,
True love forever that always lasts.

Just one chance you are gifted to see
Brigadoon, the village of eternity.
Partake of goodness forever more
As you cross over the bridge of Doon.

Shrouds of mist will cover your tracks –
Brigadoon has captured your heart.
Love and kindness, all heaven's gifts
For the world you left
Will not be missed.

Build Your Walls

Build your walls,
Your fence of steel.
Make them high
With barbed wire tops.
Use your fortunes
For patrolling cops.

Keep your cameras
Working night and day.
Let the guard dogs
Loose at night
To give those beggars
A horrific bite.

But wait a minute,
This is me!
The pensioner,
The underdog
Who wants to see
Just how rich
Some shitheads
Can really be.

Cardboard Street

Look in your city,
Your town or your street.
Look for the cardboard
That rises at night
To shelter the homeless
On a cold windy night.

From all walks of life
These box dwellers come,
The sick in the mind,
The frail and the weak,
Cardboard and paper
Are homes they all keep.

Cornflake or porridge
As long as it fits
Their bodies at night
In the parks or the streets.
They line them with paper
As much as they find
And pray to their god
That the weather is kind.

The drip of the rain,
The roar of the wind,
The sound of their heartbeat
When huddled within.
Sleep is not easy
On a cold winter's night

When the frost and the snow
Threaten frostbite.

Night air is bitter
When craving for sleep,
Especially when raining
And the box starts to leak.

The box is all soggy
And falling apart,
Time to move on
And find a new home
Of cardboard and paper
And a cold pavement stone.

Cast Off the Veil of Doom

Cast off the veil of doom.
Condemn this self-pitiful tune.
Think positive in these trying
Days and chase those blues away.

Paint a picture in your mind
Of love and beauty of many kinds.
Give a thought for those in need,
Cast off those shrouds of greed.

Lend a hand to the desperate ones,
A kindness shown by almost anyone.
Give love and kindness in these dark
Forbidding days of foul money sharks.

If by chance a money fool you meet
Whose selfish ways are indiscreet?
Just grab him by his knackers now.
Squeeze them until you hear a pop,
A voice sounds like screams from hell
For you have changed his sex from boy
To girl!

Cerne Abbas Giant

Come dance you maidens
In the cool of the night
Within the ancient grounds
Of Cerne Abbas Giant.

Virgin brides in Celtic times
Saw the Dorchester chalk man
As the ultimate fertility rite.

They would climb the hill
When the sun went down,
Shedding their garments
On the chalk Dorset ground.

Praying to this symbol
As they pranced around,
Praying that phallic giant
To give fertility to the womb,
The blessings of children
That would be fathered soon.

Cherish Your Freedom

Cherish your freedom that you have won.
Don't surrender it to anyone.

Blood was poured
Onto barren earth
So the common man
Could cast off his chains
But the marks of servitude
Still remain.

Evil forces are at work
To take away your freedom gained.
Fight them, beat them at their evil game.
Don't let them take freedom's name away.

Cold Weather Payments

Cold weather payments –
What a load of balls.
The old just freeze to death,
Just clogging up the morgues.

Am I just a cynic?
Can this be really true?
Con-Dems want us all to die
Before a payment gets to you.

I do not trust a single one.
Westminster makes me sick,
As dirty stinking politicians
They know all the rotten tricks.

Strip them naked in the freezing cold.
Let their knackers turn black and blue
Then break them off with catapults
And use for dumpling stew.

Collective Amnesia

So the world went bust with banks and
Institutions the people no longer trust.

Trillions are missing and we've been
Deceived by crooks and politicians with
Their hands in the till who preach austerity
From the pulpit of greed and haven't a clue
Of what are our needs.

'Tighten your belts,' these crooked ones
Spout but never talk justice that surely must
Come for the bankers who stole from
Each and every one.

Find those trillions these fat cats took
For they are lowest of all the common
Crooks, lower than scum, the dross of
All human ones.

So if the talk is cuts and austerity days,
Let's cut the wealth of the grossly overpaid.
Take off the blinkers that keep the amnesia in.
Check and look for OUR money you
Crooks have all lent.

Come on Back, Oliver

Please come on back,
Oliver Cromwell.
We need your sword,
Your iron fist, to cut off
Their hands from their
Stealing wrists,

To run your sword through
MPs' guts and crush their balls
And sterilise their nuts,
To slash off fingers that
Steal our cash and to clear out
Parliament of this cancerous trash.

Come back, Oliver, and do your best
To rid our country of these pests.
Make them pay for what they have done
To the commoners of England,
The downtrodden ones.

We have the rich, the elitist ones
Who rule the nest as King Charles
Had done. They bend the laws
As he once did and they treat us
Poor as serfs and pigs.

Clear them out from the halls of shame
And rule this country in Cromwell's name.

Give the people in England's fair land
A Parliament of the people and not

The chosen few. We hope you will put paid
To them and run these bastards through.

The Stone of Destiny

'Tis Longshanks the Scots do fear,
King Edward, the butcher of Welshmen,
The lanky king, with English spears.

The King of Scotland Edward said,
So doing battle in Perth, he stole the Stone
To rest in Westminster for the English throne.

You can have a king to rule in my name,
John Balliol, the puppet king.
Edward just sat back and pulled the strings.

But tempers flared in Scotland's realm.
Battles were fought, both near and far –
Berwick and Edinburgh to the town of Dunbar.

Then William Wallace, a wealthy landed gent,
Took umbrage with Longshanks, the English king, and
Did battle at Falkirk, to be soundly beaten.

Some years later, Wallace was found
Hiding and skulking in Highland glades
Then executed for treason by Longshanks's blade.

For many a century the Stone did stay
A symbol of dominance under England's name
Then returned to Scotland from whence it came.

Crazy Humans

As the chimp gazed into
This cold lifeless skull
Empty eye sockets
Stared back into space
This human creature
Did once embrace.
This crazy human
Missed his cue
When nature said

'Cease what you do
Your time on earth
Is about to end.
Your destructive ways
We do not defend.'

But they heeded not
What nature said.
Now all human life
Is stone-like dead.

So we chimpanzees
Now rule this world
And read the books
From the human time,
All that they
Carelessly forsook.

Darwin's lessons
We read and browse:
Don't mess with nature

Or alter its course
For it will kill you off
Without remorse.

Cry Burma

Freedom went
So long ago.
Democracy died
Along with the state
Their leader and mentor
Aung San Suu Kyi
Tried to create.

Evil tyrants
In khaki dress
Fired the bullets
Into human flesh,
Ripping out freedom
With chunks of lead
As monks and nuns
Lay dying and dead.

A puppet state
Of China
Next door,
The Generals
With soldiers
They employ.
But forty years
Is far too long.
Military rule
They can't defend.

China must make
This nightmare end.

Cry Freedom

I cry for freedom
To speak your minds.
I cry for justice
For all humankind.

I shed the tears
Of sorrow and grief.
I care not for your
Religion or beliefs.

I shout compassion
For those who suffer.
I denounce oppression
Of one another.

I am a human,
No mystic being.
We have no god
Just one another.

I cry for freedom
Each day I wake.
I beg mankind
To cast off his shroud.
I implore him
To just look around.

I can see mankind's
End in sight –
No god or magic,
Just nature's might.

Daddy-Long-Legs

They called him
Daddy-long-legs
A long time ago,
Just skin and bones
Where flesh should grow,
A long time ago.

A diet of bread and dripping
Or fatty breast of lamb –
The kids of Britain lived on this
Throughout this war-torn land.

Clothing came from scarecrows,
So the story goes.
His shoes were full of gaping holes
And cardboard kept them dry
But not the cold from winter's snow
When ice did melt inside.

They called him Daddy-long-legs,
His limbs were built to run
Away from bombs and poison gas
His nightmares and the Hun.

Skinny little matchstick boy
His ribs were plain to see.
I know this little skinny kid.
That little waif was me.

A Conversation with Dave Allen

I was talking the other day to Dave Allen.
Yes, I know he
Is dead but we are kindred spirits as far as the 'other
Side' is concerned and you might just
as well believe this
story as anything else in this world. This is the
Story he told me when he spoke to God.

Now just a minute, God,
You just listen to me.
Stop giving me that crap,
You've just failed in your job.

And don't tell me you tried
To block my hopes and fears,
Don't tell me anything else.
You're supposed to be God.

Are you telling me a porkpie?
That life will surely change.
You've had 2,015 years
For this miracle to arrange.

Peter, with great respect to those
Who are still waiting for something
To happen, may your god go with you.'

Devil Yellow

This yellow metal we call gold,
The curse of man since times of old,
Untold misery it creates
When mankind succumbs
To this yellow hate.

Man will kill his fellow man
For just one handful
Of this yellow sand.

Devil yellow with its evil glow,
The curse of man
Wherever he goes.

Hypocrites of the religious faiths
Preaching the gospel to a poor man's face,
'Give your coins, so you're forgiven'.
In the name of their god
They do their bidding.

Did Jesus Christ ask for gold
When forgiving man
For deeds untold?

Precious metal sealed his fate –
This was the beginning
Of the yellow hate.

Donate your gold for a front-row seat
To be near the god you wish to meet.

But what a shock awaits you and me
When the Day of Judgment comes to be.

You will find no golden throne
Of priceless jewels and ermine robes.
You will find a humble seat
On which sits a being
You cannot CHEAT.

Do They Give a Tommy-Tit?

I've got this pain
From my fingers
Going down
To my toes,
Painful as hellfire
But not many
Of you know.

Take this pill,
The quack
Will say.
Take the lot,
Just fade away.

They don't give
A tom-tit
Or even a fart
If the old git
Is in pain.
Just swallow
These pills
And GO AWAY.

Just a fart
In a spacesuit,
As unwelcome
As that
When seeking
Medical help.
For in Britain
It's crap.

Doctor Mengele

This poem is my answer to the person(s) in this right-wing government who proposed last week that the older generation should not be given the chance to recover if their life is in danger. I have chosen the one character in history who would relish this undertaking, Dr Josef Mengele, the Angel of Death – but remember, this is pure fiction!

Doctor Mengele is alive and well,
Employed by the NHS, for just a spell.
It's found itself short of cash.
Mengele said, with an evil smile,

Leave it with me. Let me have a bash.
I can save you millions of NHS cash.
Kill the over-60s who clog up the queue.
Turn them into 'Soylent Green'
As clean as a whistle, so nothing is seen.

Give the money to Thatcher's Kids
Or the sick little BASTARD whose idea this is.
I can end their life at sixty-one
Regardless of all the good they've done.

This world is for us chosen few
Not for old farts to clog up the queue.
We have ways of killing, making them die
And turning them into delicious meat pies.

We put their corpses into mincing machines,
      Add a few herbs, for that final taste.
You haven't a clue you've eaten GRANDDAD.

Be on your guard, you old crinkles. Watch out for
      Someone with salt and pepper pots.

Dog Eat Dog

It's dog eat dog in this poxy world
That has become all the rage in Britain's
Land of shame.

When MPs, who graft and cheat, and
Greedy bankers, the lowest of scum,
Human scumbags, which soil our streets,
Legalise wholesale robbery from
Everyone who breathes and speaks.

Big fat bribes pass from hand to hand
As lobbyists and crooks dish out the loot
To elected pigs this nation should shoot.

Dog eat dog as they strip off the flesh,
The money and wealth, till nothing is left.
Throwing the bones to the weak and the poor,
Cutting all the benefits and ramping up the rent,
Cheating the workers till they are sixty-seven.
Work till you drop and your life is all spent.

Pigs of greed could not care less for the disabled
In mind or the crippled in pain, mothers with kids.
A choice of heating or eating? They don't give a fig
As dog eats dog in the land of corporate pigs.

So watch for the bloody backlash that is stewing away
That's making the entire workforce into serfs of
corporate Slaves.

As the nation will rise and throw off its chains,
Slaughtering the scum who make them eat dirt,
Remembering the poll tax and the riots that ensued,
Burning the symbols of the capitalist bums
And building a new England for everyone.

Dog eat dog will never be when the people rise up
To chase out these thieves.

Don't Cut Down the Forests

Don't cut down the rainforest
And burn down the trees'
Life-giving foliage
In the high canopy.

Remember the creatures
Who lived in these trees,
Destroyed by the flames
For man's selfish greed.

But nature is powerful
As all humans will see
When it rises to strike
Those who cut
And burn these trees.

A blight on their land
With flooding in depth
As the forest is no more.
It kept the waters in check!

Don't Grow Old

Don't grow old in this uncaring world where
Society cares little, or even understands.

The world has fostered the septic ones who
Care so little even for their own dads and mums.

A product of greed, all the children it
Deceived, just telling the kids that there is no society.

There are cretins and maggots who rip off
Their own for a pound or a dime or two then
Tell the old that they cared for you.

You pay these arseholes to look after someone,
To give them the care in their twilight
Days, but they rip off the old in diabolical ways.

Paid by the state, in a lottery draw, the
Lowest bidder and the shitehawk ones win
The contracts to fleece these elderly ones.

In ten minutes or less their staff must rush
To clean up the elderly and make up the bed,
To make them a meal and see they are fed.

But the truth must be told in the light of day,
The mess of the urine, the stench of the
Detritus that's messed in their beds and the
Crumbs they are given to say they are fed.

Millions of old all over this world are too scared
To even speak for they suffer in silence till
Death heals their pain and the bastards who
Did this do it all over again.

Prosecute and castigate the whole ruddy lot.
Sling them in prison for the compassion they forgot.
Give them the care they give everyone
and see if one of YOU would wipe their bums.

Down Hardship's Road

There is talk in Britain of the people
of this nation having to
Carry the can for the misdeeds of the
rich bastards in this corrupt land.

Bankers and the City scum have got
away scot-free with
Billions of pounds of the people's money
and the establishment want
Pensioners to have their pensions cut in half
and child benefits
To be stopped altogether and all of our
wages to be cut by
30% to pay for their stinking fucking ways.
Well, bollocks to the establishment, kiss our ass.

Down Hardship's Road politicians told
us no hard truths that we
In Britain would pay the cost of corruption
and theft by City
Scum who wiped out this nation by these
foul-smelling bums.

We, the people, must pay with our wages,
our pensions as well,
As the rich and elite of the grand upper
crust look down on this
Nation as Britain goes bust.

We must walk down Hardship's Way whilst bankers,
The robbers of Britain's wealth, languish in
luxury with the cream
From the top as the majority of us are left to rot.

Give up your pension, your benefits too,
and join the end of the handouts queue.
Don't look for a job for all those have gone.
Don't look for hope for it's never in sight,
but get ready to battle in the forthcoming fight.

Riots and mayhem are just down our
road when arseholes called politicians,
The establishment class, get out the
whips to kick our ass.

But here is a warning to the upper crust,
the detritus and scum
Called the ruling ones – don't go down
Hardship's Road any night
Or any day for the people of Britain
will make you fucking pay.

Down Life's Highway

To love each other is the only way
In a world full of horror, every hour, every day.
Love one another, with hugs and a kiss,
This gentle gesture that no one would miss.

Give loving words straight from your heart,
Tenderness and caring every new day you start.
Cherish the memories of departed friends.
Open a fresh page, deep in your heart,

Inscribe it with love, of the life that they had.
Their memories are safe and will never depart.
Clasp the hands of the lonely ones,
Fill them with love like a summer's sun.

Don't cross the road when a beggar you meet.
Give generously to them, that food they may eat.
Care for each other each hour of each day
For this feeling is catching
Down life's highway.

Dressed in Black

Dressed in black and an ice-cold look,
The meter man withdrew his book.

Smirking as he passed my way,
'Got you,' he hissed at me
As he wrote out my details gleefully.

'What's up, doc?' I say to him,
'Can't you see that badge within?',
As I put both crutches under his chin.

'I lost one leg and the use of one arm
And the army gave me this adapted car.
So book me now, you fascist crumb
Then pull this crutch from your BUM.'

Gee, this really got my wild up.

Eleven of Eleven

On the eleventh day of the eleventh
Month and on the eleventh hour
A minute of silent remembrance.
Gathered at the cenotaph, rich
Powerful hypocritical two-faced
SHOWER.

Not one of these great and good
Took up arms to defend our lands.
A fascist king of the Windsor tribe
Did his best during World War Two
To sell our lands to Hitler's crew
And slaughter the non-Aryans and
The Jews.

Just one minute is all that they get
Of pious words as wreaths are laid
To the warriors of war, our sons and
Dads of years gone past, as the government
Of the day stand there in their sombre suits,
But the truth be known couldn't give two hoots,
Doing nothing for the veterans who are left, who
Languish in poverty until their deaths.

And when the sanctimonious have done
Their bit the real heroes of that day march
In the thousands with medals gleaming bright
To honour their comrades who paid the ultimate cost
That keeps the elite in well-paid jobs.

So stuff the establishment and its inverted snobs.
Get rid of the monarchy and the divisions it makes
Of a class-ridden system of 'them' and 'us'
And pay the dues owed to veterans
Before they turn to dust.

Emma

Please look out for my little dog,
I ask all those who believe in God.
I did something I never do.
I prayed to God to keep her safe

But he never heard. He never will.
Emma is dying, maybe soon,
But there is no god for animals
For that's a fact.

There is no money in dogs or cats,
Your stinking Bible tells us that.
But if you're lucky on your journey's end
Please look out for my beagle friend.

Tell her I love her and always will.
It won't be long till we meet again
And we will roam forever in the
Woodland glade.

For my constant companion and beloved friend.

England

'Tis my native land,
My place of birth.
The English language,
My mother tongue,
We gave to many
Nations on this earth.

This tiny nation
With a lion's heart
Spanned the world
From shore to shore.
Our brand of democracy
And fair play
Are the hallmarks
Of the English way.

Science and commerce's
Written and spoken words,
Descriptive and flowing
In noun and verb,
Great men of science
And the literary kind
Used our English,
Our mother tongue,
Writing like Shakespeare
Books for everyone.

We are proud of the soil
Beneath our feet.

My home for centuries
This fortress we keep.

Our customs and ways,
Our food and drink,
The flag of Saint George
So proud and distinct.
Many a foe has failed
On history's battlegrounds
To conquer and enslave
The English to no avail.

We are of Anglo-Saxon stock,
Viking and German.
It's in our blood,
With Roman and Celtic
In our genes –
Truest warriors of England
That were ever conceived.

Welcome you all
To England's fair lands.
Sip our cup of kindness
And well-mannered ways,
With centuries of hard-won
Culture for all to partake.

BUT taking us for granted
Is your biggest mistake.
English blood
Was poured onto
Strange foreign shores

To create this England,
A homeland
That makes England great.

Bring tyranny and ridicule
To the hard-won
Freedoms of English ways and
We will cast you adrift,
Bound for the Stone Age
From whence you came,
To fight your own battles
As the English have done
To create another Eden
From whence they come.

Epitaph for Mrs T (Version 2)

This poem is dedicated to Mrs T when and if the witch ever pops her clogs.

The day will come
When the witch is dead
As all good Tories
Must bow their heads.

As they write the sermon
To praise this evil one,
And the Britain she created –
No society or class
Just them, not us,
Unwashed working class.

Praise be to railways
That we once had.
Long live the thieves
Who stole our gas.

All the utilities
That made Britain great,
She sold them off
One by one –
Power and riches
To her Tory chums.

Let's build a raft
Proper and fit with

Props from the mines,
The disused pits:

Wooden poles,
Her body lashed to them.

Tow it to sea
Way out of sight.
Just like the *Belgrano*
We will sink her at night.

Pinned to the raft
As it sinks all alone
A note from the bitch:
Please forgive me.
You were sailing home.

Eternal Love

How long does love last without a beginning or a past?
This feeling in one's heart was always there from the
Very start for every man who walked this earth
There was a woman who gave him birth.

That's why love will never die for man
is part of woman.
True, for out of woman he came too
for man and woman
Who fall in love ride a chariot to Venus
the goddess of love,
This star that's never dimmed, forever
fed from our love within.

Just look at love as the stars above,
as centuries of lovers
Who have parted this world beam down
their love in A magical spell.

To capture two hearts in a heavenly embrace, till death
Do they part this mortal race – wondrous love,
You mysterious thing, the one good part
Of our very being.

So ride your chariot to that Venus high till the
Centuries pass, young lovers – Bye.

For long after our bodies rest we will share our love
Amongst the rest.

It's in the heavens where you gaze,
that you will find your
Love in this wondrous haze.

Eternity Star

We technicians, the unsung ones
Who devised and made things come true
So our boss, the doctor of physics
Could pinch it from you.

'Test them all till they fall apart.
Give me the best, and data too,
So I can claim all the kudos from you.'

But we never cared for he was our friend,
David, the scientist, the PhD,
He was the boss of Phil and me.
A seven-year project with successful end
But cancer killed our laboratory friend.
We miss you, David, with your bearded smile

And your beguiling ways in those seven-year trials.
May you become that star we talked about.
Save a place for Phil and me
When we start on our journey
To eternity...

Eton, the College of Division

Built in 1440 and founded by Henry the Sixth,
A school for kings and other landed rich pigs.
Built with class distinction as the guiding rule
That will view all others as knaves and fools.
Walpole to Cameron and Osborne, the foul
Ones, this college teaches elitist division to
Everyone. The sons of crooks, sharks and
Barons and kings taught how to debase their
Fellow man with impunity.

As the dross and drop-outs from inbred sick
Marriage, they are taught the detritus from their
Arse does not smell. Serfs and plebs can use
This waste matter as toothpaste.

Arrogance is inbred in all who enter this college
Of division. Sons of those who robbed this nation
Blind and the offspring of a feudal monarchist
System that is in need of desperate revision
Or elimination in its totality are moulded into
Useless lumps of humanity by tutors of Latin
Who themselves must shoulder the responsibility
Of producing the scum and dregs of humanity we
Call the establishment.

Eton should be demolished, brick by sordid filthy brick
And the land it stands on ploughed under to the very
Last inch, then covered in pig-pens to
remind the nation

And its peoples of the greedy pigs
who were brainwashed
To believe they had the God-given
right to rule us.

Snobs and arrogant civil servants
in and around Westminster
Who are the product of an Eton education,
and hence the class
System, must be driven out of Parliament
and its halls of
Corruption and their cursed motto of
'We were born to rule'
Buried in the history books of British infamy.

Evil Is That Evil Do

'Tis evil the witch
That makes this brew
To cast the evil
Spell on you.

Carefully planning
In the coven nest,
The warlock
Spews out an evil plan
With tongue and lash
To make this
Chap completely
VANISH.

They gather
Around the
Cauldron pot
To plan the
Final evil plot.

The warlock
And his witches'
Crew pull out
The knives
To stab you
Through.

But this old
Chap is aware

Of that
As he pulls

The plug
On their
Sick trap.

He won't take
Any of their
CRAP.

Stuff you lot
And your
Kangaroo court,
Or the sickness
That this board
Has caught.

Freedom
Is a precious thing.
Censorship
Is the end
Of FREE
Thinking.

Fair Trade

They rip them off, the farmers who grew

Your cocoa pods from African plains,

Your coffee beans from Brazilian rains.

All grapes and lemons, all exotic foods

We buy in supermarkets, a treat to eat,

But think of the farmers they do cheat.

They cheat the farmers in every way

When buying their crops at starvation pay.

Fair trade to them is a dirty word.

It's all about profit margins and cost incurred.

They fleece the growers and me and you,

Dictating prices so we can eat

Food and goodies on the CHEAP.

Fair-Weather Friends

You're riding high
On the crest of the waves
In your wonderful creative
Halcyon days,

Gathering friends
(You never had),
Fighting their corner
With heartfelt belief.
They would do the same
If you stumbled on grief

But greed corrupts
And power deludes
The friend you had
With the spell
Over you.

A fair-weather friend
They turn out to be.
Your friendship is unwanted,
Way out of your depth.
Their intellect and upbringing
Just hold you in check.

So the lesson is plain –
Don't trust them again.
They want your best
For their own selfish gain.

Fireweed

A magenta flower some six feet tall
Grows in destruction where bombs did fall.
Weeds of death without a smell
Mark out spots of human hell.

Wherever mankind burns and plunders
Fireweed grows where flames have been
In towns and cities or even volcanic thunder.
Give this thought if this weed you see
Fires of death could have germinated this seed.

Note: *The author, as a child, witnessed the streets of London overgrown with this weed, just like many cities and towns in Europe after the Second World War.*

For Principle's Name

Why should we fight in freedom's name when others turn their coward's head away?

They wring their hands and cry and shout but refuse to help the brave ones out.

Burying their heads and turning away whilst others do battle to save their soul – a perfect description of the human arsehole.

So if by chance they come your way, give them a gun and bayonet to fight or die, and say, 'It's up to you.'

Your principles won't save your life but this gun and bayonet in your hands will help defend your beloved homeland.

For The Love of Humanity

The screams of humanity just
Cannot be heard for
Thousands are buried under
Haiti's blood-soaked earth.

The poorest of peoples in this
Tiny Caribbean state which in
Decades past the rich and
Powerful did always forsake.

No oil or wealth for these rich
Pigs to steal, only humanity
They used as their slaves, but
That has long gone into far
Distant days.

But their blood is just red like
The blood in your heart and
They feel all the pains like all
Humans do, so dig deep in your
Pockets for that dollar or two.
Send it post-haste to the
Rescuing crews.

Around the world their cries can be heard.
Please help us in our hours of
Need and send what you can.

Please we beg, hear our pleas.

For those who still live.

For Your Tomorrow

Did the brave fighting men of Kohima die in vain
When they fought and died in freedom's name?
Do we ever think of the great sacrifices these men made
Fighting the Japs in Burma so you'll not be enslaved?

Battles of the past world wars vanish in history's dust
As we wander down freedom's road
and the bridge over
The River Kwai that slowly turns to rust.

An insidious blinding sickness infects
this uncaring land.
Many a war has gone before in barren desert sands.
Alas, all will go the Burma way of
faded memories of times
So sad.

The political elite will lie and cheat the
brave men they deceive,
'Your life in blood and sweat; your life
and death we shan't forget.'
But like the men of Kohima fame your
sacrifice will be in vain.
None of them gave a second thought
and that's a dirty shame.

'For your tomorrow we gave our today,'
Dead men shout from battle-scarred grave.
This is how we British treat the young and brave.

For my father-in-law, a veteran of Kohima who was awarded three silver oak leaves to his Burma Star – a man from Curzon Crescent called Arthur Doe.

For Whom the Bell Tolls

The dark satanic
Drone of the bells,
The teller of death,

A messenger from hell,
They toll for us –
The whole human race.

The bells of destiny –
Our final disgrace.
The greed of man
Makes these bells ring.

We cannot hide
From the chill they sing.
All life will cease
When you hear
Their death ring.

Four and Twenty MPs

Four and twenty MPs
Baked a money pie.
When the pie was opened
The MPs began to sing,
'This is the loveliest money
dish we have ever seen.'

Then all their families
Came out to play
With the money from the pie.
They ate and ate
Until they were full of
The money belonging
To you and me.

'Now that's a naughty thing to do,'
All the other MPs shout.
'Why on earth did you not tell us
So we could dive in with our snouts?'

Free Fall

In the world
Of the deaf and dumb,
Does Mr Brown
Know what's going on?
Blinkers as shields
Won't hide the truth.
Labour is crashing
Through the roof.

For Mr Brown
Is deaf and dumb.
He can't hear
The shouting
Going on.
He won't utter
What we want
To hear.

Drastic socialism,
A change of course,
Dumping big business
And PFI without remorse.

Speak out and tell us –
Are you not a dream
Or just a myth?
A leader of no one,
Or a blundering fool?
Or is greatness

Soon coming
As Labour
Free falls?

The folly of Gordon Brown, PM.

Free Speech

I was bound and gagged,
Not a sound was made.

My world went dark
As state censorship invades,

Twisting the knots
That gag humanity tight.

Having sleepwalked
Into state control overnight,

I woke with a scream,
Opened my eyes, a nightmare dream
As I realised that FREE speech
Was being denied to me.

Our freedom to write
And speak your mind

Is going forever within
Britain's shoreline.

Just a dream (or is it)?

Freedom

Freedom is what men and women
Have died for over the centuries.
The freedom to talk and write
Without fear of persecution from state
Or any narrow-minded person or group.

Freedom is worth fighting for.
Without it we slide down that
Terrible slope towards
Dictatorship and oppression.

Freedom is the will and ability
To say what YOU think is
Right and wrong
Without fear of some
Dictator saying otherwise.

Freedom is the right of all
Men, women and children,
Regardless of creed, colour,
Class or breeding.

Those who suck up
To the oppressors
And dictators of our basic
Human rights are just as guilty
As those who carry out
And foster this injustice.

Funny and Cunning

How funny and cunning
Words can be.
They can hoax us all
Into what to believe.
They can go and on
Ever to deceive.

They can spin a story
To gather sympathy
That fools other readers
To create empathy.

But strings of lies,
Deceitful untruths,
The fodder for tykes

When the truth is
Unveiled
As reality bites.

Georgie Osborne

Georgie Osborne, pudding and pie,
Robbed the poor and made them cry.
When the unions came out to play,
Georgie Osborne ran away.

But Dell Boy Cameron of the Eton mob
Told young Georgie to zip his gob.
Keep it quiet, so they won't grieve,
So the nation won't notice all we thieve.

Georgie Osborne, pudding and pie,
Started to steal from you and me,
Robbing the poor to keep the rich,
His Tory principles long ago ditched.

Then young Georgie of the Eton crew
Asked his mentor what he should do.
Thatcher screamed at pudding and pie,
'Kick the disabled until they die.
Make the whole of Britain out of work.
Get on with it, you stupid jerk.'

Then the riots and burning in the streets
Forced the coalition into a fast retreat.
A general strike did its work
As the nation kicked out these stupid jerks.

Ghostly Tales of Cornish Ground

Near the tavern of Jamaica Inn at Bolventor on Bodmin Moor, the ghost of a murdered sailor of ancient times is seen in moonlight on the stone-brick walls, cursing the devil who caused this all.

But at the Dolphin Inn down Penzance way, Judge Jeffreys, the Hanging Judge, did sentence to death on the gallows tree a captain of navy and sailors three, smuggling rum in barrels so big the whole of Penzance did dance the death jig, as drunk as a lord when they hung up the four but their mates cut the ropes tight round their necks to escape Judge Jeffreys and start smuggling once more.

Stranger still is the tale from the Punch Bowl Inn at Lanreath, a stone's throw from Lostwithiel and the mad black demonic cockerel which you can still hear crow, as it flies through the night, screeching as it goes.

In Boscastle's Wellington Hotel many a ghost has cast its spell – the coachman dressed in leathers of black who wanders through brick walls this way and that and the serving wench of a bygone age who threw herself from the roof of this inn to be near to her lover, the coachman in black who walks through the walls, this way and that.

There is the phantom coach down Mevagissey way, four horses and driver on a four-wheeled coach, who vanish into thin air the moment they approach but barrels of rum and brandy most fair cascade from the coach before it goes up in smoke, so smugglers, they say, from Truro's fair town chased

By the peelers for stealing the rum, but free drinks are the order from these barrels of fun.
There's yet another tale from the Cornish ways but, my friends, I will tell you on another day.

Give and Take

A story appeared on the box about the price of the new cancer drugs. One must be a millionaire to afford these drugs but then I dug deeper into the story (as you do). After contacting the cancer charities we give to on a regular basis (standing order) I was shocked at what goes on with OUR money.

We British are a generous lot
Giving to all those charities
That sometimes are forgot,
But did you know the hidden truth
Of where your money really goes?
It goes to your local university
Researching how human cancer grows.

YOU fund the bulk for all those years
So science can say it 'knows'.
We've found the cure for this and that
But we must not shout 'Eureka'
For there is a great big catch –

Greedy little pharmaceuticals
Will truly make sure of that.
Greedy pigs will take what's given
And PATENT in their name
The cures that you and I have paid for.
Now that's a disgusting shame.

They brand as their very OWN
The drugs you know will cure
But charge us till we are bankrupt
These drug firms from the SEWER.

Global Warming

In a secret leaked government
Brown paper, a committee of
Cross-party MPs have come up
With an eye-watering idea of how
We can halt global warming.
The very thought of it makes
My eyes water.

To save our planet
We must trap our farts.
We must wear
A gasbag on our backs.
All farts exhausted
MUST be trapped.

We will have a pipe
Stuck up our bums
And this must be worn
By EVERYONE.

When you go to bed
Or have a bath
You must have this pipe
Up your arse.

Cheating the rules
Is NOT aloud
For fart-smelling dogs
Are on the prowl.

This inflammable gas
Will heat our homes
And power our cars
When we want to roam.

We must eat baked beans
By the bucket load.
Be sure to empty your bag
Or you'll EXPLODE.

The national grid
For discharged farts
Will empty our bags
For a fresh new start

So tuck in well
To your baked bean snacks
And fill that gasbag on your backs.

Globalisation

Such a nasty word to baffle the poor,
A creeping cancer and a festering sore
Destroying this world with the ultimate sin

Of enslaving humans for the stinking rich,
Their morals and principles long ago ditched.

They will tell you and have you believe
This is globalisation, and it has to be,
But when is enough ever enough?
How much wealth does one man need?

When the obsession for money turns into greed
From India to China across all seven seas,
The bandits from the West come to deceive.
Chairman Mao would turn in his grave

If he saw his peoples turned into slaves.
Gandhi would rise from the dead
If he witnessed the morsels his people are fed.

Women and children are turned into slaves
As the dollar almighty digs mass graves.

Why is it called the Third World?

God Help Me

'God help me,' cried the African woman
who nursed her frail child in her arms until
he died.

Where was your God?

'God help me,' screamed the millions
who heard the gas chamber doors
slam shut.

Where was your God?

'God help me,' cried the untold millions
who have suffered torture since the days
of the Inquisition.

Where was your God?

'God help me,' shout those who suffer
unspeakable pain through illness.

Where was your God?

God is an illusion
Made in man's mind.
He's come in many shapes
Throughout the course of time.
No soul has ever come back
To tell the world it's true.

Blind faith has no meaning –
It corrupts and deceives you.

All things turn to dust.
In the four winds we will blow.
We will fertilise our little Earth
Into new things we will grow!

Amen.

*These are some of the reasons that I became a
committed atheist because religion is the cause of most
wars and hatred on this sorry earth.*

Grab and Gobble

Grab and gobble all we perceive
We are the Maggot's children of greed.
Stuff you lot, who gives a toss?
The Maggot's philosophy rules. She is boss.

It must be us always, first and last.
The rest of you can kiss our ass.
What we see is what we get
For we are the Maggot's chosen ones.
Who gives a fart for you stupid bums?
No such thing as human society,
The Maggot said, as she preached
Her dream.

But now this evil has come home to rest
As the Maggot's kids lose their nests
For negative equity is here to stay,
Worthless houses with giant debts to repay.

Blame the Maggot for this mess you're in.
She preached the sermon that 'greed is everything'.
Greedy fools now in their forties follow that dream
As the bailiffs and banks skim off your froth and
cream.
You had it all, the world was yours,
But your greed and selfish ways
Made the rest of us poor.
So stuff you lot, who gives a fig?
For you greedy pigs never did.

Greed is Good

What's all the fuss about? Some clever
Twit stole half the world's loot. So what? So
What's the big deal? They can print some more
So the rest of us can steal some, can't they?

Greed is good for you. It makes you fat and
Lazy but it helps to keep the workforce
Turning over. Sack the first lot then hire the
Next lot at half their pay – now that makes
Sound greed sense.

Put up the mortgage rate to 50% per day –
Now that makes good greed sense. Turf
Them out if they default on a penny of our
Hard-won stolen money, then offer them a
Rented tent on the lawns they used to cut at
A minimum rate of 500 bucks a day. If they
Default, burn the ruddy tent down. Now that's
Sound greed sense.

Put up the price of everyday foods, bread,
Milk, coffee, sugar etc etc till the masses are
Starving hungry, then double the price of
Everything. Now that sounds like greed
Sense.

Do not pick up the dead and dying you find
Littered over the highways and byways. The
Plague and other deadly diseases are good

For greed – double the price of the vaccines
And medical care. Now that sounds like good
Greed sense.

All bills and daily food rations must be paid
For in CASH. We do not trust plastic or banks
Or government promises. Now that sounds
Like good greed sense.

All communications with us greedy bastards
Will be conducted by cell phone at premium rate,
Charges of ten cents a second, or in the case
Of the UK, ten pence a second. NO reverse
Charge calls will be allowed, even from our
Own granny. Now that sounds like good
Greed sense.

All phones will be hired from us at the ultra
Low price of fifty bucks a day, with a two-
Thousand dollar deposit upfront. Likewise, a
Premium will be paid to us for walking on
Clean dead people, free
pavements (sidewalks), at a price to be agreed.
Now that sounds like good greed sense.

So you see, greed is good for you, as long
As you never ever get caught. The
Consequences are too horrible to think of. So
Far I have seen ten sets of men's ball bags
Hanging from lamp posts in one street alone.

Grenfell (acrostic poem)

Grieving heartache that never ever stops.

Repugnant inaction we have not forgot.

Endless tears that just flow and flow,

Nothing but nothing will end this so.

Flames of passion and a burning hate.

Establishment blunders are belated.

Love and anger go hand in hand

Looking for justice in a divided land.

Grumpy old Gits

I made my wife promise me that she would shoot me if ever I got this bad. This she did gladly (with a smile).

Grey old men with stubby faces,
Bad-fitting teeth, when in place.
Grumpy old gits with Victorian ways
Who curse and jabber in their waking days.

'Get off my lawn,' you hear him rasp
Should a child's ball land on his grass.
'You miserable git,' the young ones shout
Which makes old stubble-chin dance about.

'I'll tell your parents what you've done,'
As he waves his Zimmer at the little ones.
'If I was them I would spank your bum,'
As he stumbles and mumbles after one.

'How much is that?' the old git says
When out shopping with his pension pay.
'Fifty pence for a loaf of bread!
You must be joking,' in a rumbling rasp.
'You can stick your loaf up your arse.'

'Just look at that,' you hear him say,
Should a gorgeous woman pass his way.
'You dirty old git,' the young girl says,
Wiggling her bum at his lecherous gaze.

Never wrong when he states his views,
Always better than me and you,
He will always argue till the cows come home.
Black is white or the Earth is flat –
The silly old git will argue with that.

'What's his name?' I hear you say.
Will, Tom, Phil, Dick,
Make your choice, you take a pick.
You put the name to that grumpy old git.

Half a Century of Love

'Tis the ode to our love of half a century long
Of the beautiful young lass of sweet seventeen,
Satin skin that pearls would grace, bewitching
Eyes of emerald green, smiling, beguiling voice
Of this angel's face, this half a century has just
Embraced.

Love and passion of a purest kind, caring, sharing
Throughout the years through joy and sadness
Uncountable tears have marked our love forever
More on the journey we made on paradise shores.

We crushed each other in a heavenly embrace
Not a soul or living thing could ever and never
Come between a love so deep and meaningful.
The gods in heaven rained down their love
To seal this dream in eternity's dreamland
Space.

So over the course of a very long time, our love
Is as strong as when first we met, as eye to eye we saw
Our dreams mapped out forever more of two humans
Who so adore that little look, a knowing glance of a
love
That time has so well enhanced.

Hands

This poem is about our hands, the most constructive and destructive parts of the human body.

Mankind will (if he is lucky)
Inherit the universe
And his hands will play a major
Part in this exploration
But they will also destroy him
As sure as night follows day,
Unless he learns to live
In harmony with his fellow man.

Look at my hands,
So clean, so bright,
Not a scar or stain in sight.
Hands so young
No work you've done
But wait, my fingers,
Your days will come.

See them soon
When you start to work
Pulling handles
In a factory's dirt
Or manual work
On a building site
Splitting your hands
Till blood-red bright.

Hands so cold,
Chapped and sore,

Heaving coal
For a fireside roar
For in the 'pits'
You might be
Working deep in misery,
Pick and shovel
On your back,
Hands and body
Midnight black.

Two strong hands
Might kill and plunder
If your country calls
For military thunder.
Gun in hand
You pull the trigger
To kill and maim
A human figure.

See them later
In years to come,
Puffed up veins
Through all the strain,
Blackened nails, full of grit,
Hands and fingers
Bruised and split.

But see them now
Your work days done,
Twisted joints,
Wrinkled skin,
Sinews withered,
Bent with age

Now you've reached
Your twilight stage.

Served me well,
My hands once strong,
Earnt my living
In workdays long,
But look my hands
At what you've done
Throughout the lifespan
Of us human one.

You built this world,
For some it's heaven,
Then you press a button
For Armageddon.
This world you made
Will blow to bits.
You see some hands
Do EVIL tricks.

He Had Seen It All Before

He had seen it all before since a lad from the Second World War – man's inhumanity to his fellow man, From Hitler to Stalin to Ho Chi Minh,this man has seen the inhumanity begin.

From the gas chambers of Belsen, these chambers of death,
To the trains to Auschwitz that brought in the Jews
To die in their millions in this endless queue.

The slaughter of Barbarossa in 1941 – Hitler invaded the Russians in a blitzkrieg attack, 600,000 Russians were slaughtered in that. But all in all over 55 million died for the evil of one man, who told his nation lies. From 1949 to 1976, 40 million died in China's vast lands when Mao Zedong created a Communist state, a dictator that no Chinese could escape.

Then there was the Korean War, north and south, Soviet-backed Kim Il-Sung invaded the south to the Dividing line but the world said, 'Stop', before a Third World War began. Nearly three million died Fighting that war from all over the world on these foreign shores.

From the Congo to the Khmer Rouge and Afghanistan, the Soviet War, millions have died fighting these Pointless wars. Nearly five million dead. What the hell for? Iran-Iraq in deserts they fight, just one million are dead – tribal traditions to prove who is right.

Vietnam and Cambodia this old man has seen, and wars for the arms magnates to make the few rich, to Wipe out whole nations, to kill millions and more, bullets by the billion, ten cents a score.

In memory of the needless killing, I grow weary of needless slaughter.

Headless Chickens

The election's over.
Labour went bust,
With MPs ranting
'We have lost their trust.'

Flapping around,
Chickens without heads,
Our seats are lost,
The party is dead.

Blaming Tory Tony
Or Wee Goody Brown
As the whole of Labour
Came crashing down.

'What went wrong?'
The numbskulls shout,
Forgetting the DEAD
From a distant war,

Forgetting the underclass,
The wretched poor,
Forgetting the old folk
And forgetting what Labour
Really stood for.

Heed the Cry of Anger

Listen to the wails of children's pains of hunger.
Heed the people's cries of the nation's pent-up anger
As they shoulder the burden for deeds
they have not done,
As conservative scum pillory the underclass ones.

The sickest, vilest government in recent British history
Using us, the underclass, to pay for banksters' thievery.
They rob the poor to placate the rich,
stinking Tory gits.
The disabled are robbed blind by these fleas and nits
Who the poor class them as the detritus of septic shit.

*Note: I can see another poll tax time of riots
and burning of establishment buildings all over
Britain because not a soul in this far-right junta is
listening to the masses as they fight a losing
battle against austerity that was conjured up by a
Conservative government that hates all things working
class, but the odds are stacked against this junta
because we are many and they are the few.*

Hi, Said Electron

Hi, said Electron
As he went around,
Have you seen Proton,
Charged to ground?

Yes, said Atom,
You're part of my core.
We three are brothers
And that's for sure.

Not so quick,
Neutrino said,
As he nudged old Quark
From his bed.

We are subatomic
Like you three.
The Neutron giggled
And Lepton slept.
Don't wake him up,
That's a dear
Or time and space
Will disappear.

Don't be silly,
Higgs boson said.
They plugged me into
That accelerator machine.
Quark and Lepton

Are black holes
In space and time.

Strings and things
Are all sublime.

(Simple cosmology)

Hindsight

If 'hindsight' could be bottled
List the things you wouldn't do.
Take a sip of bottled 'hindsight'
To release that curse on you.

But 'hindsight' can't be bottled
As every human knows.

The mistakes you made along
The way will go on haunting you.

But the biggest lesson you will ever learn
Is not to love or be loved in return.

Hollow Words

Hollow words is all we hear, of jam
Tomorrow but tears today, the promises of
Better pay, of fairness for all, one sunny day.

Hollow words is all it is for our world
Is controlled by big business, whose only aim
Is the bottom line of a balance sheet and
All the tax they can cheat.

Hollow words for the underdog's corrupt
Politicians just fob them off then promise the earth
On polling day, then do nothing as the years
Roll by as the poor ones just fade and DIE.

So hollow words don't mean a thing as they
Trip off the tongues of lying human beings.

How Deep Are Our Pockets?

Deep in the bubbling cauldron
Of mire swim the thieving leeches,
The detritus of the upper class
Passing wind and fire.

MPs and lords belching out their shit,
Pay your taxes and we can pinch it.
We have a moat chock-full of crap,

Dry rot in my lover's distant flat.
Our ducks need housing in the pond,
Porno of bondage tied up with thongs.

Phantom mortgages on ghostly pads
Double our money, now ain't we a cad?
We paid our mortgage years ago.

Pretend we never see the cash grow.
High walls of steel and electronic gates
Keep out the voters who just irritate.

Wall to wall TV and computer screens,
Bath plugs and dildos and sexual things.
Put it on expenses and let's rip away.
They're parts of the perks of the MPs' pay.

How Green is My Valley

As rough as nature intended,
A beauty that your eyes do see.
Breathtaking in all its glory,
Bathed in a gentle breeze.
Air as sweet as mayflowers,
Song birds that nest in trees,
Green are the meadows
Of my valley,
Something
You all
Must
See.

How Long is Eternity?

How long is eternity
Without a beginning
Or a mortal past?
How long is a heartbeat,
One pulse that never lasts,
Just the flicker of an eyelid?
That's how long forever lasts
So close your eyes and open your mind
Whilst I take you on a journey of a magical kind,
Riding on a rainbow, across the Milky Way.
We can stay there forever more
Till the end of days.

How Time Flies

The first fragile breath
Of a newborn's cry
As into this savage world
A child must survive,

Fighting the odds
Of hundreds to one.
This child must develop
A keen sense of worth

To battle the unknown
On this hostile earth,
To learn to live
And suffer the loss.

Love and rejection
That's its very own,
Fight its corner

With a mirage of foes,
Some of its family
And some all alone.
Time is its enemy

For time will not stop
The relentless ticking
Of Father Time's clock
To make its mark,

A place in this sod.
'I've been here.
This is the hole
Where this human stood.'

Human Greed

Grabbing, grasping, despotic things,
Repugnant bipeds are human beings.
Evolution has fostered this nasty trait:
Everything is mine, the rest must wait.
Despicable humans even hell placates.

I Am a Human

I am Genghis Khan and Attila the Hun.
I am all these creatures who massacred
The human ones...

I am Adolf Hitler and Stalin too,
Joseph Goebbels who butchered Jews
Or Idi Amin the Ugandan despot
Who murdered his people and ate
Their flesh, this African monster
The world forgot...

I am Mao Zedong and Pol Pot too
Who massacred their people in
China's vast lands, the same in
Cambodia with the Khmer Rouge...

I am all of these, rolled into one
That your God almighty called
The human ones, for he is
Your likeness, the image of you
So he must be a monster
Just like you!

But on reflection, this cannot be.
This world is not as horrible
As I paint in this prose.
There are some good humans
As to their whereabouts
Knobby knows!!!

I Am the Reaper

Come, pay your dues.
You had your chance
To make amends
For the carnage
You've reaped,
My earth-bound friends.

Pay the ferryman
As you board his boat,
Telling you tales
Of the afterlife,
Rowing the lake
The devil forsakes.

But I could have a word in his lughole
And get you a better deal for 700 billion dollars.
I could find a cooler place in hellfire for a few.
Just give me the nod and wink and the deal is done.
Please contact me at the following address:
Lucifer Stakeholdings Inc, Wall Street, NY.
Leave all your worldly possessions with
The Reaper before you contact me.

I Am the Wind

I am the wind
And rain
That wets
Your face
For I am
The lifeblood
Of the human race.
For I am YOU,
You are ME.
We are as one
In this human tree.

I Hate This Firkin Country

You have to be rich to keep your pet
When you pay a ransom to a vet.
The councils think you're a money tree
Then squandering it so recklessly.

Gas bills have gone through the roof.
Just like the dentist bill to pull a tooth.
The electric man is a great big laugh.
They rip us off, they think we're daft.

Trains are for the super-very-rich.
Virgin and Co have their hands on it.
Water meters don't give a toss.
You pay by the pint, so you don't wash.

Petrol prices are an obscene vulgar joke.
God bless BP, may the bums go broke.
Pensioners go cap in hand in every corner
Of this firkin pigsty crapheap land.

MPs wallow in fantastic wealth
Stealing our money, the nation's pot.
Put them in irons and shoot the lot.
I hate this firkin country, the stinking lot.
The Maggot was better than what we've got.

May Brown go down with this sinking ship
This septic firkin Burke can take Blair with it.
I've seen enough. They make me very sick.
Rip off Britain, you sick firkin gits.

I Heard Eccles

I heard Eccles the other day,
Moriarty and Bluebottle.
'Twas the yearly ball,
The annual advent of
Lord Snotdon Crapper
Of Crapheap Hall.

On the guest list,
The Goons one and all.
There was Eccles,
The giggling twit,
Moriarty and Bluebottle,
The sleuth and nit.
Major Bloodnok
And Griptype-Thynne,

Ned and Minnie Bannister –
All were quite sublime.
Spike and Peter,
Harry and Mick
Had the event in laughter
With their daft slapstick.

Ghosts from the past
From the radio days,
The austerity times in
Britain of 1949.

In My Woods

I was in the woods
With Emma my dog
When nature called
Before I wet my togs.

I wanted a pee
As we men always do.
'Twas far away
From gazing eyes,
Not a single human
Would see my flies.

Was nearly drained
From this normal thing
When a ruddy great voice
Came a-BOOMING.

'Stand still, you bum,'
These speakers did hum.
'We are the Council.
You can't pee in here.
Stay where you are
And do not run.'

As I looked up
Into the high canopies
A mass of CCTV
Is all I could see.
Tannoy speakers

Camouflaged with leaves –
Big Brother gone nuts

In England's tall trees.

So if I wanted a crap
How would they react?
As they got a glimpse
Of my bum the devils
would laugh at the
Tattoo on my arse.

I Will See You

I will see you in the stardust
On the journey we all must take.
You will see me on a moonbeam
Or in the bright twinkle of a star,
Flitting and skipping to galaxies afar.
Turn your eyes to the heavens above.
Look at the stars that twinkle at night,
People we knew all laughing in delight.
They have found that nothing ends.
Our soul and mind will travel on –
New beginnings with dear
And loved friends.

If Only

If only: sad words of the past,

Regrets and sorrows of a bygone age.

If only is too late, the deed is done,

Actions not taken to save a loved one.

If only we knew, if only we had seen,

Life would be different, if only had been.

In My Mind's Eye

I would purge evil from the soul,
Eradicate the need for greed,
Give the world the means to feed,

Banish all religions based on hate,
Stop the brainwashing of little ones.
Bigots and tyrants we must eliminate.

Start again with the political class.
Wealth and privilege is not the key
When we choose the people
To represent you or me.

Take the pain from the mother's eyes,
Never to see another child die.
Take the torment from the human brain,
This hell on earth that drives them insane.

In my mind's eye, all this I see.
But in truth this is far from reality.

In My Woods

The tiny snowdrops have gone away.
Just once a year their heads do sway.
Amid the bracken on woodland floors,
These miniature daffodils live once more.

This little replica of the sunshine plant
Just as pretty as normal daffodil giants.
Its yellow flower slowly bobs and weaves
Within a shroud of vivid green.

Mystic tales surround these miniature ones
Sprouting their heads in a March-time sun,
Giving protection to elves and fairies in the night.
Tiny flowers that will close when darkness breaks,
Sheltering elves and fairies until morning wakes.

It's not a breeze that makes the daffodils
Dance and swing. Just look and listen carefully
As little ones jive and sing.

Thank you, golden daffodil, you made us safe
In a nice warm bed away from spooky woodland
Grass in which sinister creatures lurk and want us
dead.
But tucked up warm inside your bell, we live and
Weave and sing and cast our spells.

In Sickness and In Health

They say that like attacks like in many of life's pathways we wander down. My pathway to love has given me fifty-four years of love with the most beautiful girl in the world, whom I love and cherish deeply. This poem is about both our eventful times and tribulations on life's highway.

I've travelled this road, ages long,
Born to a family where I did not belong.
A stupid mistake that I was born
In a loveless world, full of hate.
Black sheep, they did not relate.
Twenty years in this mould,
Deeds of cruelty yet untold,
Married a girl I truly love,
The life she had was no dream –
Dominant father with bad genes.
Those genes are in the family tree
Which surface and erupt frequently
But I've witnessed cruelty at first-hand,
Her blighted past I understand.
Our love is stronger than a wayward gene.
We cast them aside like a nightmare dream
For the vows we took when we wed
Remain with us till both are dead.

In the Beginning

'Twas a void of nothing in the Viking world
Called Ginnungagap that lay to the north
Of Niflheim, a dark void of thick fog and ice,
Firepits of Muspelheim like a dragon's mouth
Flaming like the volcanoes deep within the south.

Niflheim was plagued by intense cold and ice.
The spring of Hvergelmir created the seven rivers
Flowing to create the Elivager ice floes ten miles deep
Until it met the hell of Muspelheim with molten lava,
Fire and brimstone as ice and water blew the land apart.

In the Midst of Greed

Do we really understand what has happened? Can we comprehend the magnitude of the disaster that has fallen on those who had no part of in its making, and the suffering that has
Befallen them?

Greed on a scale that has never been seen in this world before Has struck the whole planet senseless. Banks of all manner of Sizes have declared themselves bankrupt.

Some of the world's most famous institutions have gone bust Overnight, leaving a mass of bad untouchable debt. Wall Street And London stockmarket institutions are under investigation for Corruption and wholesale theft of the world's wealth.

The weak, and poorest of nations, are left to flounder in the mire Of global corruption and the those who are defenceless amid this Storm of daily revelations of pure unbridled greed are left by the Wayside to perish in the rubble of worthless houses.

But those who played no part in this calamity that has broken the Back of the world's financial system are earmarked to pick up the Tab of those who by all common justice should be in prison.

The poor and downtrodden will pay the price of this wholesale Global greed; this includes most of the world's pensioners who in Britain are on or below the official poverty line. Their paymaster Sees this group as an easy

Touch, a despicable form of government that cares little for its old.

New Labour is now in its death throes; the last of its spinning is Nearly over. Its lying and cheating of the pensioner will cost them Dearly come the next election.

But a fearful beast is primed to unleash itself onto the frightened And bewildered British nation. The BMP will gather all those disgruntled and disillusioned downtrodden pensioners and gain Power up and down this land of ours.

So in the midst of greed, seeds are being sown of a racist and Nationalistic nature for the blame game will not be on the Shoulders of greedy bankers and stockbrokers, but the BNP
    Will point their vile fingers
    At those from other parts of this world and make them the
    Scapegoat for what happened and what will follow next.
    New Labour has ignored the hands of help from its core support as it
    Tends to the needs of the greedy and corrupt bedfellows.

In Whom We Trust

Some trust their dads, their mums,
Others trust their daughters or sons
But life has taught me, beware of everyone.

Do you trust a politician to tell the truth?
These slimeballs of the upper crust,
Just like the dentist who pulls your tooth,
They rip us off till we go bust.

Don't put your trust in religion's way.
Have never seen the dead rise from a grave.
It never stopped six million Jewish people from dying.
Did any religion whatsoever hear their cries?

The trust you have is what you see.
Trust your wits and none will deceive.
Beguiling words, trust none of these.
Nature has fashioned the human gene
But this 'trusting gene'
Has never been seen!

Infinity

Was it love or lust,
The primeval thrust,
These urges to blame
For into this world I came?

'Twas no fault of my own
This sperm and egg –
Be it kings or thieves
A child is conceived.

This universe was my home
But I've done my penance,
Served my earth-bound time,
Released from this carcass,
This ball and chain,

When I ride on the beast
Of Infinity once again.

I've Given Up

I've given up the deadly weed,
Coughing, and the morning wheeze.
No more fags or smelly breath,
No more puffing to an early death.

A little puff at the age of ten,
Roll-up fags as we called them then –

Players Weights,
A Woodbine or two,
State Express
Or Craven A,
The finest cigs of their day.

I've smoked the lot
In years gone by,
Now it's time to quit
Or I will surely die.

I'm chewing gum
And sucking sweets.
I've stuck on patches
From my feet to my tum.
I've even stuck some on my bum.

It seems to work,
The urge has gone,

But now I'm addicted
To bubblegum.

I say hello to friends I meet
With a bursting bubble
Stuck on my cheeks!

Jack and Jill

Just a little observation on the drivers of today!

When out driving in your streets
You're kind and courteous to all you meet
But have you met the ill-mannered ones
Who lower their clothing to flash their bums?

There's Two-Fingers Jack and One-Finger Jill,
They put up two fingers or a lone middle one,
Shouting obscenities, with sneers or a grin,
'Spin on this, you stupid old bum.'

Watch out for women, these bundles of fun,
Speeding along on the daily 'brat run',
Cursing and jabbering, because they're late
To pick up the kids from the local school gate.

With flailing of arms and hooting of horns
These monstrous women have no manners at all.
It's 'Up you, Jack' or 'Spin on that'.

These bats out of hell on your local racetrack
But there is a Jack or Jill in everyone!
Just push the right buttons
To see if you're one.

Jerusalem Hymn

And did we all in post-Cameron times
Walk upon England's crime-free streets
And was the holy NHS free in England's
Pleasant pastures seen?

And did we countenance evil times
That blighted the poor and ill,
Shined foul upon downs and hills
Amongst these dark satanic Tory bills.

Bring me my rifle, that Enfield 303.
Bring me my bayonet of desire.
Bring me my bandolier of bullets to fire.
Bring me my tank of steel-track tyre.

I will not cease this mortal fight
Nor shall my rifle sleep in my hands
Till we have rid our Jerusalem
Of Tories from England's
Green and pleasant lands.

Sorry, John Lennon

(Reply to his song 'Imagine')

I'm deeply sorry, John,
It was never meant to be –
This imaginary world
You made for you and me.
They still think there's a heaven
But hell on earth is the true reality.

You imagined
All the people
Living for the day –
Sorry, John, this cannot be.
There is no equality.

You imagine
There are no countries,
No religion too.
Let me tell you, John,
We are plagued
By both these two.

Greed and hunger
Is still with us.
It never went away.
Millions have died
In Africa since
This song you made.

We never had a brotherhood
But we have the greedy man
Who kills and plunders
All he sees in other troubled lands.

You said that you were dreaming
Of a world you'd like to see
But I'm really sorry to tell you, John,
This was just a FANTASY.

With deep respect for John Lennon.

Just Dreams

In a world of fictitious dreams
Of prophets and gods
Promising all manner of dreams
Most are all lies, unattainable things.

Wake up my friends, refuse to believe
Motives, for preaching is power and greed.
My heart sinks at the genocide I see
As Darfur is dying through religious hate,
Boosting the profits of the arms magnates.

If there is a god, may he strike them all dead
But there is no god who will undo these deeds.
He dwells in the minds that religion deceives.
Just look the lands of the vast Sudan plains,
Look at these people all starving in vain.

As Stone Age morons pillage and rape, we
Can't upset the government of this lawless
State for deep in the bowels of these desert
Sands OIL is abundant for the greedy to lust.
Let the starving all vanish in a storm of dust.

Run over the bodies all buried in sand,
Get drilling for oil, the nectar of greed.
Who cares about the starving in Sudan's
Arid land?

Not many I fear will come to their aid
As oil is their god, the devil in black.
Despicable humans will see to that.

Just Follow Your Heart

One life, one soul;
Two pathways
With one goal.

Map out a course
On life's highway.
Turn to the left
Or a twist to the right.

Just follow your heart
The way to your soul.
Go down the 'right way'

Till you reach your goal.

Just Imagine

Born into a dark unseen world
No colour and depth, light and shade,
The pictures of life these eyes evade.

Just imagine –

No sounds or voices all around,
Name or language to call your own.
All the discomfort you can't describe,
The deafness of this silent world,
The sounds of life that's never heard.

Just imagine –

To speak the name of mum or dad,
Read and write and say your name,
To ask a question or sing a song,
Take for granted speech we've had all along.

Just imagine –

You're deaf, blind and dumb,
A child with all these senses gone.
Just imagine, what would you do
If this little mite belonged to you?

Just Square Pegs in Round Holes

Like a brick that makes a wall
Every course that's bound in tight,
The bricks that hold them all in place
Bind us in order as the human race.

Pecking orders we humans must all obey.
Square pegs in round holes will never fit.
'Them' and 'Us' will always be
For this is the way of all humanity.

Loathsome creatures called the human race
That nature looks on with utter distaste
But most of all on those who rape this Earth,
Stealing its bounty for all their worth.

But this stealing and raping will end one day
As the human race expands in unexpected ways.
Human beings will have no space for food to eat
For this entire Earth will be covered by human feet!

Just Wait for Me

Listen in the wind and the driving rain
Hark at my call as I whisper your name.

Go to our woods, our favourite spot,
Rest my friend in the summer's sun
Under the oaks of the spirits' run...

Just wait for me my faithful dog. It won't
Be long till we are side by side when we
Will walk in glades of spirits' woods just
As I promised that we always would.

The path we will travel in our mystic way
Will go on forever till the end of days.
Our days will be long and full of fun.
Just wait for me, my faithful one.

Missing you so much, dear Emma.
Peter, your friend in life.

Just Walk in My Shoes

I see life from
A different view –
The downside of life
Not so many have seen –
From a child of the war
To this old man of dreams.

Poverty, cruelty,
All this I have seen.
'Twas reality for me,
Never a dream.
But I grow angry
In my twilight days.
The horror and pain
Is just the same.
Cruelty to children
Has never changed.

Not just in my country
This cruelty is seen,
'Tis spread over the world.
Across all seven seas,
Children do suffer
Needlessly.

All kinds of harm
Is inflicted on kids
By carers and parents,
Uncles and aunts.

163

Unspeakable horrors
These children endure

Mostly by ones
Very close to you!

Justice

Justice is blind,
As blind as a bat.
Money and injustice
Will see to that.

Justice is a rich man's perk.
It's riddled with prejudices;
The human disease,
Making us blind
To the stark inequalities.

The wisdom of Solomon,
This mythical king,
Could never bring justice
To corrupt human beings.

Just look at your rulers
Who dish out the dirt,
Barristers and lawyers,
Real justice they shirk.

Keep Your God

Keep your God and don't preach at me.
You've been nothing but trouble since eternity.
More blood has been spilt in your name
Since Moses walked to the Promised Land.
It's a wonderful story but that's all it is.
Mankind must realise it's just a dream.
Evil things, war and death, is all it brings.

Kephalonia

Keeper of the gods' kingdom,
Empress of the Ionian Sea,
Paradise and beauty, that's what you are to me.
Heaven's golden playground, I wish it would always be.
A people of great kindness, joy and hospitality,
Legend of the ancient gods, or so the story runs,
Of gods and mortals bathing here, feasting and of fun,
Neptune's place of slumber, when basking in the sun.
I must leave you on the morrow, sadness plain to see.
Adieu, my fair Kephalonia, until I return to thee.

Land of Despair and Sorrow

Land of despair and sorrow,
A land that's full of greed,
How shall we describe you,
A land that once belonged
To me?

Born into the mouth of poverty,
They preached that God almighty
Would one day make us free
But that was just a fable
Told to you and me.

No truths or rights or freedoms
Or stars of solemn brightness
To light us on our way,
Just gloom and pitch-black darkness
In every waking day.

Land of despair and sorrow,
A land that's full of greed,
How shall we describe you
A land that once belonged
To me?

Hark, this divided nation,
This vile land of the west,
With some of great fortunes,
A pittance of the country's wealth,
Divided amongst the rest.

Our hopes are all downtrodden
By men of wealth and greed
Who ride the Tory chariot
Over every other's needs.
They plunder our tiny nation
To placate the bankers' greed,
Then force the men and women
To beg for their every need.

Land of lying bastards,
A land that's full of graft and greed,
Of governments of moral corruption,
This England of septic seeds.

(Land of Hope and Glory, BOLLOCKS).

Land of My Fathers

Scourge of my genes
That flows in my veins,
The blood of my forefathers
Of centuries past,
Bear witness to England,
The land of my breed,
This septic land
Of beggars and thieves.

From the whipping posts
Of 1694 in the dungeons
In Bedlam, the clink
For the insane,
My genes have been there.
Bear witness, my name.

'Twas back with
King Henry in 1532,
They boiled my ancestors,
My own kith and kin
For paying no taxes
On Henry's evil whim.

But this land
Of my fathers,
Like Bedlam of old,
Still manacles and shackles
And throws you in clink

For their god called money
Quicker than an eyelid blink.

For this sceptred isle
Is putrid and stinks.
For poll tax evasion
They put you in clink.

Latch Key Kids

Great Britain is at the bottom of the pile when it comes to looking after its children's well-being and the USA came second from the bottom of this list of shame. I have been there as a child and find it unacceptable that it has returned.

It's back again, the 'latch key' kids,
A phenomenon of a bygone age.
Absent parents or single mums,
All are working as the day is long.
No parents to care for the little ones,

Never at home when school day's done.
The kids make dinner in the microwave
And the eldest is the surrogate mum.
Mum is tired and comes home late.
Dads work longer for the rent and rates.

Kids are farmed out to all and sundry,
No guiding hand to keep them straight
As along life's highway, they all must take.
They open their door with a key on a string,
So cold and empty, no happiness it brings.

Latch key kids were a thing of the past
When dads were out fighting a WAR.
Mums did shift work, making SHELLS,
But Grandma and Grandpa did their bit
Giving guidance and love to latch key kids.

Logic

Give us a sign
That this story is true
Or is this carnage
And bloodshed
All down to you?

Did the wise men of old
Who created this myth
Envisage a world
Of starvation and death?

This God they created
Has never been seen.
He dwells in the minds
Of those who believe.

The image of man
Was made in his like.
Was he black or brown,
Or all shades of white?

If this is true
That he's the likeness of you
Then Hitler and Stalin
Are the image of you!

Both were butchers
Of the mass human race.
If this is the face of a God

That no one has seen
Then logic just tells you

Not to be deceived.

A wonderful yarn,
A beautiful dream,
But mankind is evil
Even those who believe.

Loneliness of the Human race

Loneliness is a state of mind,
A curse that's gifted to all humankind.

The complexity of the human race,
Our interactions when face to
Face, all our human failings
We embrace.

Acceptance of what we see and do will
Determine if this loneliness will
Cling to you.

In the midst of a roaring crowd loneliness will
Abound. It's part of the mystery of me and you.
This loneliness can be so very true.

Expect loneliness to strike one day
When your usefulness is on the wane,
When others have milked you dry
And they hang you out to die.

Kids, who wants them?

Loneliness

This poem is dedicated to all the mums in this world.
To say any more would spoil the poem.

Hello loneliness, my old friend,
Come to visit me again.

People laughing all around
But I'm so lonely in this crowd.

Faces I know I've seen,
Friends I know you might have been.

But your guile and smiling ways
Will not take this loneliness away.

I see a face that's haunting me
Of beauty and serenity.

You left my life so long ago
But the flame within can't let go.

I wear a mask that no one sees,
A mask that hides my shattered dreams.

I would lay down my life for one chance to say,
And banish this loneliness far, far away,

'Thank you, dear Mother, for all that you've done.
You're still loved by us all, each and every one.'

Look at What They've Done

Just look at what this government has done.
Five years of hell for the working-class ones.
This sickness of mind that was last conceived
By Germans and fascists in World War Two,
Copied by Conservatives who gave it to you.

Just like Hitler who persecuted the underclass,
Cameron and Clegg just whip and kick our arse,
Scrapping our welfare, a protection they just hate.
Zero hours contracts and working till you drop,
Retired in your nineties as your pension they rob,
Bailing out bankers who caused this ruddy mess,
Bringing in the immigrants to take away your jobs.

Millions using foodbanks throughout this Tory land,
Children sleep in hunger without the food they need,
Con-Dems made sure of this with welfare they thieve.
Millions committed suicide as disabled payments stop
Just as Hitler did by driving the disabled to the grave.
A creature called Ian Duncan Smith did the very same.

This carnage still goes on at the very bottom of the pile
As Labour sits for four years just twiddling its thumbs!
Its grassroots voters are taken to the slaughter house
When the whole of Britain shouts at Miliband to get off
His bloody bum!

Lost Principles

In the shadows of lost principles
Within the sounds of Big Ben,
The passion and lust for change
Withered and faded on the vine
In Westminster's halls of shame.

Never a Parliament of the people
For they have lost the common touch,
For the Commons is tainted by scandal
Now big business dictates how much.

A breed of British men and women
That governs for the likes of me and you,
They call themselves honourable MPs
But the roundhead, Oliver Cromwell,
Would simply run them through!

Mascara and Tears

I watch in wonderment at this magical trick
As you curl your eyelashes, twist and a flick.
The spell is cast in your mirror of dreams
That transforms you completely
My beauty queen.

You turn to face me from your make-up seat.
Your angelic smile turns me quite weak.
A single red rose on a thorn-free stem
I take from a bunch where I've hidden them.
'This is for you, my darling, my dream.'

As she clutches the stem in her tender young hands
A tear wells up in her sea-green eyes, rolls down her
Cheek on to her dress where it lands.

A single black mark is etched on her cheeks,
Mascara and tears in a jagged black streak.
'You fool, you wonderful fool,'
She laughed and she cried,

As she dabbed the last tears from her beautiful eyes.
'Look what you've done to my silly old face.
Mascara and tears in all the wrong place.'

We hugged and kissed in a passionate embrace.
I whispered, 'I'm sorry for spoiling your face.'

We never went out that long summer's day.
The bedroom was home, our lovers' nest.

You know what we mean.
Thou must guess the rest.

Me and My Shadow

My constant companion, my faithful friend,
Your eternal presence will never end.

Standing there at the tip of my foot,
Stretching and shrinking with the wane of the sun,
You've always been with me since my life began.

Casting my image in a myriad of ways
From an infant in diapers to these halcyon days,

My shadow and I will never depart
Until six feet of earth drives us apart.

Me and my Shadow (2)

I run and leap,
Play hide-and-seek.
My constant companion,
My faithful friend,
Your eternal presence
Will never end.

Standing there
At the tip of my foot,
Stretching and shrinking
In the wane of the sun,
You've always been with me
Since my life began.

Casting my image
In a myriad of ways
From an infant in diapers
To these halcyon days,
My shadow and me
Will never depart
Until six feet of earth
Drives us apart.

Me Old Granddad

Old granddad
Smoked a pipe
Like his friend
The blacksmith.
Shag tobacco
Gave both delights.
Ready-rolled
And ready-rubbed,
Player's Digger Shag
Was Granddad's
Favourite one.
With a penny
I would run a mile
To give old Granddad
A contented smile.
Murray's Erinmore Flake
Was Mr Davis,
The blacksmith's, take.
When he and Granddad
Smoked as one,
The sweetness of the aroma
Delighted everyone.
They puffed and jawed
Through a smoke-filled fog
With briar pipes in their gobs.
Lighting up, now and then,
When pipes went out
And just jawed again.

Mirror, Mirror

Don't lie to me.
Is this image really me?
What has happened
To that child-like skin?
Who is that wrinkled old has-been?

Mirror, Mirror,
Is my hair really that grey
And will these wrinkles go away?
Are my teeth that brilliant white?
How come they leave my mouth at night?

Mirror, Mirror,
You've seen me all
From childhood days
To this silly old fool.

Mister, Can You Spare a Dime?

They used to tell us
To save for that dream.
So we saved all the time.
For once we had a bankroll,
Now it's gone.

Mister, can you spare a dime?

We saved like crazy
To realise our dreams,
Saved a fortune
In dollars and dimes,
Then the sly crooks
On Wall Street
Suckered our dreams.

Mister, can you spare a dime?

For once we trusted bankers
With their towers in the sky.
Once we trusted bankers,
Now they've gone.

Mister, can you spare a dime?

Once we trusted governments
To come to our aid
And save our nickels and dimes.

Once we trusted politicians,
Now that's gone.

Mister, can you spare a dime?
Peter, can you spare a million or two?

Monetary Violence

Build it high, vast mountains of cash
Becoming the shepherd to tend the flock.
Keep them moving like clueless sheep
Grabbing your money for banksters to
Keep.

Using your money to keep you all in check,
Just one of billions who are part of the flock.
The masses are clueless of the yoke around
Their necks.

You work for 'them' whom nobody has seen.
Empty your pockets of all that you had
As lambs to slaughter they pick you clean.
Banksters are crooks and subhuman beings.

Greed is their master that you must placate,
Working forever and paying your way,
So banksters grow fat on half of your pay
Then shear off your coat and the grass
That you eat,

Kick you and whip you till you are half dead,
Dole out a pittance to the lambs and the sheep
Then slaughter you all, as a feast they will eat.

The violence of bankers is a sight to behold
As cold as a TURD in an ice-bound pool.
Evil bastards, one and all.

Morality's Demise

For the love of money and the cures of greed
Oxford and Cambridge taught many a thief.

Devoid of all morals that encompass most of us,
Philosophy and economics of the upper crust
Create crooks and criminals nobody will trust.

Economics of the fabulous stinking rich,
Who worship the gods called oil and gold,
Set for life at the top of establishment tree
As the rest of us just die in austerity's freeze.

Educated bankers, the greatest of thieves,
Who stole a king's ransom from stinking RBS,
Letting the rest of us plebs clean up the mess.

No embarrassment of the deeds that were done,
They pocket massive bonuses for robbing everyone.
Set for life in his eagle's nest as he sticks up two fingers
At the downtrodden rest.

So off to the hounds he rides his steed, and a tally ho
As his hounds yelp and bay, killing
himself with laughter
At the billions YOU will pay back
for this educated snob,
Who came from the wilds of Oxford or
Cambridge and didn't
Understand ruddy JOB.

Morality and caring is never taught at high schools.
They leave that for the rest of us
cause they know we are
Stupid fools.

Mother of Mine

As a child, I do remember
The mother of mine
As an infant tender.

This wonderful lady,
So frail and so weak,
Who gave her life
For her children's keep,

This beautiful lady,
We called her, Mum,
Who was loved dearly
By her daughters and sons.

This wonderful woman,
Who is sadly missed,
Who made us better
With a tender kiss.

A proud little woman
In shabby old clothes
Who brought us up
Through our troubles
And woes.

She did without
So we could eat
And put the shoes
Upon our feet.

This precious woman
With the heart of gold
Who never complained
To her little fold.

She never treasured
Silks or laces.
She found it all
In her children's face.

For this lovely old mum
So old and so grey,
I would lay down my life
For the last chance to say:

'Thank you, dear Mother,
For all that you've done.
You are loved by us all,
'Each and every one.'

Mother

My mother was a leading woman in Hitler's Third Reich. She was the first woman in the German Waffen SS and she held the post of SS-Aufseherin Lilly Wicks, Iron Cross with Oak Leaf,

But she was so wicked even for them that they kicked her out.

Hitler himself paid for her to be parachuted back into Britain

And to re-join her kids in the kitchen of Woodvine Cottage.

That was a sad day that Lilly stormed into the house,

The clank of her hobnail jackboots as she goose-stepped into the kitchen and gave the order to 'Stand to attention, you swine.'

SS Lilly did her bit for the Fatherland. At night she would shine

A torch at the German bombers to direct the bombs onto our house in the hope they would score a Direct hit, thus freeing her for the German war effort. Hitler had promised his Iron Maiden that if he won the war she would be put in charge of all the PINK SALMON in Britain, but alas he lost the war and Lilly went into hiding with her youngest daughter and ten tons of tinned pink salmon.

But she was caught red-handed one day as she ran to the hardware store for a fresh tin opener.

A story of survival.

Mr Bush, Are You Firkin Blind?

For The Ontario Coalition Against Poverty.

We were told to build a dream,
A dream that we would all share.
My brothers and I did the hard slog,
Built the roads and tilled the land,
Raised the skyscrapers to the gods.

We did the things that were asked of you,
To plough the fields and plant the corn,
Take up arms to Old Glory's songs.
Brave Americans just joined the throng.

Now we are waiting in breadline queues
Begging for food for our kids to eat,
A few dimes for shoes on our kids' feet.
'Mr Bush, are you firkin blind?'

Once there was a war in desert sands.
Dressed in khaki with a Browning gun,
Gee, we were soldiers, brothers and sons
But many died and many were maimed
In Uncle Sam's glorious name.

Now we wait in breadline queues
Begging for food for our kids to eat,
A few dimes for shoes on our kids' feet.
'Mr Bush, are you firkin blind?'

Gleaming medals cover our chests
The cost of two hamburgers at the best.

A Purple Heart or a Navy Cross
Enrage young men with limbs now lost.
Stuff your medals, give us food
And give us the dignity
For those who would have died for you.

Now we wait in breadline queues,
Begging for food for our kids to eat,
A few dimes for shoes on our kids' feet.
'Mr. Bush, are you firkin blind?
Is that all you can spare, a firkin dime?'

Inspired by Bing Crosby with his 1931 hit song,
'Buddy, can you spare a dime?'

Mrs Brown Has Guinea Worm Fever
(Western names are used to make it easy to understand)

I see Mrs Brown
Has Guinea worm fever
And her husband
Is going blind with trachoma.
They say a deadly
Mosquito plague
Is at our doors
But malaria or dengue fever
Don't bother me anymore.

This is Africa.

Poor Mr Jones is riddled
With leprosy and his kids
Are dying with the deadly
Ebola bleeding disease.
Shame his wife is sick
With Cholera
Or is it Yellow fever?
Both are as common
As chalk and cheese.

This is Africa.

Tuberculosis is rife.
It killed Mr Green
And his wife.

Their kids went sick
With diarrhoea.

Or was it dysentery?
Passing blood instead
Of stools they never will
Go back to school.

This is Africa.

Mind you, we've seen worse
With polio and rampant AIDS,
Sandfly fever, with the threat of SARS,
And elephantiasis
That made the Johnson
Twins' limbs so enlarged.

This is Africa.

We had a dose of whooping cough
An outbreak of measles too
But not as bad as Marburg fever
And that tetanus,
By the gods, that killed quite a few.

This is Africa.

This puts us all to shame.
How dare WE complain
When we suffer a dose of flu?
Put yourselves in Africa's place.
See if these deadly diseases
Would kill off you.

Mrs Mohawk Spock

None human, with your pointed ears,
Having the power to overcome our fears.
Power and passion within your gaze
Dwarfs all emotions of the human age.

Your hands make love within our heads
When you mind-meld with your hands
Passions and experience we can't understand.
Beauty and orgasmic dreams that no human on earth
Could ever conceive.

Murdoch

Murderer of free speech wherever this creature goes,
Uncaring for the freedom of others, this
beast has made it so
Rancid as a pile of kangaroo dung.
He feels at home with that.
Dead and not buried yet, he spouts
his selfish evil creed
Of brainwashing all the world for
loot for him to thieve.
Creature from the cesspit of all the nations'
running shit,
His name is Rupert Murdoch,
his newspapers are soaked in it.

My Faithful Friends

When I look back to distant years my
eyes fill up with emotions'
Tears. I remember my faithful friends
from the pups they were
Till the journey's end.

My dogs and I – bound by love of
these trusting ones, my
Constant companions through the
tempest of life, a gentle lick
For they knew best.

They sensed my sorrow of life's
hard knocks, a nuzzle and a
Cuddle and that knowing look for
they sensed my grief and the
Tears I shed when told a dear
one was now quite dead.

There was Floss and Jemma, Cherry
and Emma, who is alive
And well, the beagle bitch of lemon
and white who chases the
Hares in the bright moonlight, getting old,
just like me, as we
Wander down this highway to our ultimate destiny.

When the day has come when I reach for
the stars, my wish is
For my girls, my faithful friends, to wander
with me on that journey so far.

My First Kiss

Lift the veil so I might see
Those big green eyes of emerald green.
You cast a spell with a heavenly smile
With lips of ruby you do beguile.

Soft satin skin with the touch of doves,
Perfume from heavens of which I love,
Hair as black as ravens' wings
That shimmers in the light.
Dimpled cheeks each time you smile
And teeth as white as Arctic snow
That sets my heart and soul aglow.

A heart of pure beaten gold
As precious as wealth untold –
I fold you in my longing arms
And touch your face with tenderness.

To melt into one, my very first kiss
As two hearts beat the rapture of love,
Blessed by the heavens and stardust above,
We start on the journey, a lifetime of love.

My Mind's Eye

Deep within us all is a secret
Place only YOU can visit –
A place so secret that
It has no name
But my mind's eye.

Within this fantasia world
YOU are the ruler of all things.
My mind's eye can cure
With just one look
All who suffer.

Injustice has no place in
My mind's eye
For I am Solomon.
To feed the masses
I take from the rich
And give to the poor.

Robin Hood is my brother –
My mind's eye makes this so.
I am Odin and Thor
As one warrior against oppression.
Amongst the savage beasts
Of this world
We are but brothers.

Fearing no evil force
Or bowing in reverence to

Any god-like creature
For in my mind's eye

I have the power
To right all injustice.

I have the Hammer of Thor
In my hands, as Odin looks on.

My Tin Bath

A galvanised tub
Made from steel,
This hung on the wall
Until bathtimes did fall.

Oval shape, and some were round,
Just two-foot deep from end to end
Filled with water from copper pots,
They boiled on fires till bubbling hot.

We took our turns, the seven of us,
To take a bath once a week
With carbolic soap and scrubbing brush.
The one called Mother was in her glee
As the brush drew blood so wantonly.

Washing soda was used a lot
To remove the scum from of us kids
As one by one she bathed us lot
In that bath of torture I've not forgot.

National Service is Coming Back

All lads of eighteen
Must join a queue.
National Service is on its way,
A two-year service with little pay.

Sixteen weeks of drill by numbers,
You quiver in your socks
As the drill pig thunders.

'Get your hair cut, you dopey twit,'
As he roars in your ear, dribbling spit.
You wake at five to a bugle call.
Your human rights mean nothing at all.

'Get out of that pit,' the drill pig shouts,
As he tips the beds of the sleepyheads.
Just ten minutes to do this chore,
Wash and shave under coldwater taps.

No doors on loos when you have a crap,
Bedblocks made when fully dressed.
'Get on parade,' the drill pig shouts.

You run onto the square to join the rest
Up and down and round and round.
You know every inch of that ruddy ground.

Shouting numbers each step you take,
The rebel's spirit the drill pig breaks.
You learn to march the soldier's way,
A lesson well learnt on your two-year stay.

Nature's Glory

Have you ever seen a bluebell wood,
Nature's event on a yearly display,
A carpet of blue in the month of May?

Have you ever heard a skylark sing?
High in the heavens, you hear their song,
Impossible to see as they dart along.

Have you ever seen a field of corn
In a gentle breeze, or a gusty storm?
A land-based sea of yellow and green
Like the ripple of waves in a stormy sea.

Have you ever sniffed the fragrance of hay
When it's cut and baled and drifts your way?

Have you ever seen the hare and rabbit run
Early in the mornings for play and fun?

Have you ever listened to the buzz of the bee
As it gathers the pollen from plants and trees?

Have you ever touched the leaf of a tree
So silky and cooling in a soft summer breeze?

Breathing out oxygen in the hot summer sun,
The lifeblood of all creatures
Each and every one.

Negative Equity

In modern folk of the day
It's the natural thing to say,
'Me always, first and last.
The rest of you can kiss my arse.'
It's 'Me now' and never you
As they push and shove
In the smallest queues.
If there's two of them,
They grab them both.
You're just a silly joke.

'That's for me,'
As they push and shove,
Grabbing and gobbling
All they see,
Leaving the rubbish
For the likes of me.
Designer posers
With imitation kids,
The four-wheel drive
With the selfish streak,
Respecting others
Like farmyard pigs,
Up to their necks
With massive debt.
Just laugh at it
With scant relent
Was negative equity
Just a dream,

Something the 'Me-Me's'
Have never seen?

The bubble burst
For the nouveau riche
In the darkest days
Of the late eighties.
Our pork-bellied friends
Have yet to see
The disaster that comes
With negative equity.

Never

For those who will never come back.

Never heard the bullet
That smashed my brain,
Never saw my blood-
Soaked grave.

Never did see
The river of blood
I gave this country
That I loved.

Nor did I see
A promise come true
Of truth and justice
For ALL of you.

Did not see
My widow's face
When told about my fate,
Or my kids grow up
In the bosom
Of a welfare state.

Never saw my widow's pay
Or the work she did
To make ends meet
To put the shoes
On my kids' feet.

Did I give my life for nothing?

Was it all in vain?
Tell me when you see me
Things are not the same!

Nightmare Dreams

Beat me into a soggy mess.
Fists splash my piss-soaked vest.
The daily ritual has just begun
As the brute of a mother
Beats her thirdborn son.

Bloody hand marks weals on skin,
Marking the body where
Callous hands have been.
Bleeding nose and swollen lips,
This evil woman knows all the tricks.
Stay away from school this day.
If the school board see this mess,
The police would knock,
This woman they'd arrest.

Kicked and abused, the odd one out,
'Nigger lips' or 'Rubber lips' my
Other siblings did often shout.

This young child knew a thousand swear words and
Sticks and stones did break my
Bones and names did really hurt me,
And love was never seen in this house of
Nightmare dreams.

Left to die in a coal cellar black when German
Bombers did attack, the screams of fear saved
His life when the air raid warden heard his cries
Then handed him back to the mother who hoped
Her thirdborn son would have DIED...

Nod and Wink

Do you know Nod and Wink
A shifty pair who graft and cheat?

Brown envelopes are their calling cards
Stuffed with cash or big fat cheques –
Just enough so you don't forget.
In every village and every town
Nod and Wink can be found.
In the Commons and the Lords
Nod and Wink lay out their stalls.
You want some cladding for your flats?
We supply the cheapest crap.

For this and that a price is found
When Nod and Wink are around.
You want a tank? A battle ship?
Nod and Wink can supply it.
You want our NHS, its very soul?
Well, go to hell you vile arseholes!
This is OURS and not the YANKS'.
Now piss of back to the United States.

Greasy palms and grubby hands,
Thieving, stealing grabbing gits,
Nod and Wink know all the tricks.

You want our houses,
Our council flats?
Well, go to hell.
You cant have that.

The poor in Britain
Are bleeding poor –
Not always like this,
That's for sure.
A war was fought
Till late 1945
When men and women
Bravely died.
On return to Blighty's shores,

Their former life they would not endure.
Class distinction was alive and well,
Establishment and privilege was once more.
The election came in '45 –
Labour and socialism were alive.

They pledge this nation
Those things must change.
No more ownership
By the richest few
But everything owned
By me and you.

Nationalisation
They called it, then.
Public ownership
Of everything –
Fuel and power,
Phones and gas,

Mines and shipping,
The whole razzmatazz.

The NHS came to be
That gave free health care
To the likes of me,
A dental service
Free to all,
No more money
For teeth to pull.
A pension book
Labour did pledge,
Paid from the profits
Labour now said.

But along the way
Things did change,
Mrs T did arrange.
She STOLE it all,
The nation's wealth.
Her filthy hands
Were everywhere.
She stole the milk
From little kids,
Sold our water
As well as gas,
Essential elements
We must have.

No more profits
For everyone,
No more pensions

That nationalisation
Was meant to pay.

The rich and powerful
Now have the sway.

We've come a long way
Since the socialism of '45
When Labour was powerful,
With real men of steel,
Not like the fungus –
This gutless crap
Just like a Tory.
Blair and Brown
Made sure of that.

Not For Sale

This Earth of ours
Is not for Sale.
Your greedy ways
Will not prevail.

We make you rich
Beyond your needs
Then you pretend
You're deaf
To our dire pleas.

But we, the people
Of this Earth,
Will not surrender
To your global wealth.

You can't pollute
The air we breathe.
You can't rape
This Earth of trees.

You do not own
The sun that seeds
Or the sea
That breeds
The fish we eat
Or the very soil
Beneath our feet.

We are the people
Who make the rules
Not you bloated
Corporate fools.

The day of judgement
Is on its way
When the peoples of Earth
Will have their say.

They will strip you NAKED
For all to see,
The fat bloated bellies
Of corporate GREED.

Not Me, Guv

'Not me, guv'nor,'
Wall Street bays.
'We keep a few billion
For OUR rainy days.'

But trillions have gone
To pay off bad debt
Wall Street stockbrokers
Would rather forget.

They smirk and jibe
Behind cupped hands
As American taxpayers
Pick up what's failed
To bail out these cretins
Who should go to jail.

Republican greed,
The Conservative way,
Blame it on Main Street
As they huff and they puff
But the American people
Have had enough.

'Not me, guv'nor'
Won't do anymore
As the sharks from
Wall Street
Vanish from the
Trading floor.

Now Is The Winter

Now is the winter of this old one's time
When feet do freeze and chilblains tease
And grandkids now as tall as me.

Long past my three score years and ten,
Born witness to mankind's evil ways
Fearful of his demise and end of days,

So, I pass this message on to you:
Forget your colour, black or white,
Cast your religion to the winds,
Destroy wealth that makes you sin,
Just live as one in the human race
Find your gold in your kiddie's face.

Work as one, let your love unite,
Steer a course that's straight and true,
One that takes account of ALL of you
As united you stand, but divided you fall,
Wise words of old from this aged old fool.
Together you win the greatest prize of all –
Peace on earth for the very first time
When the bounty of plenty
Is for ALL humankind.

So be it be said, so let it be done.

Just A Minute

Now, just a minute, God,
You just listen to me.
Stop giving me that crap.
You've just failed in your job
And don't tell me you tried
For my hopes and my fears.
Don't tell me anything.
You're supposed to be God.
Are you telling me a porkie?
That life will surely change.
You've had 2,007 years
For this miracle to arrange.

With great respect to those
Who are still waiting for something
To happen, may your god go with you.

Nye Bevan

Nye Bevan was the man who fought tooth and nail to create the British National Health Service. If it was in the realms of reality to talk to the dead, I would say this to this Welshman, 'Nye, I had no hand in what your Labour Party has done to your beloved NHS but one by one the cretins who did this will stand before you and then you can spit in their eyes.'

Bevan would burst from the grave
If he could witness the chaos
In the NHS that he made.

They're taking it apart, bit by bit,
Flogging it off to slick city spivs,
Ripping off us all, by underhand tricks,

Paying off the doctors
That keeps them onside
As they divide up the spoils
Which they called PFI.

Asking for a fortune
For life-saving drugs,
We paid all our charities
Now they take us for mugs.

Who is making a killing
As they start flogging it off?

The traitors in Parliament
With hands in the till.

They don't give a fig
For the dying and the ill.
Nye Bevan is crying
Deep in his grave

As his cherished creation
Goes the American way.

A Pox on 'New Labour' and all it stands for
And a pox on Miliband for leading us all
DOWN THE GARDEN PATH.

Odours of Bum

I passed some wind the other day,

The silent type that smells quite neat

A perfume of fragrance, very unique.

Dog went mad but my wife said, 'It stinks.'

Analysed the contents of this silent one,

It's now on sale as 'Odours of Bum'.

Please make me happy and order some.

Oi, God

Oi, God, are you listening to me?
Are you deaf, blind and dumb?
Can't you see what your kids have done?

Oi, God, get yourself out of bed.
Get down to Africa and see they are fed.
Can't you see the hunger and thirst
On this tiny planet you called Earth?

Oi, God, are you blind in one eye?
Did you not see six million Jews
Just pass you by?

Oi, God, have you not seen
The butchery and genocide
Of the ones who praise thee?

Oi, God, it's been over two thousand years
We've waited for you. Give us a clue
That this legend is true.

Oi, God, are you a fable of old
Sold to the masses so the few could
control?

Please, God, wake from your slumber.
Get out of your bed before we all go under.

Oi, God, I think you're a freak.
You prey on the vulnerable, the young
And the weak.

Old Bess

This poem is a true story of my times. I knew and loved this horse for many years.

The old shire mare munched her hay.
She had pulled her share of coal this
Winter's day.

Along Willesden High Road to Paddington
Green, old Bess has pulled her cart, two
Tons of coal burning in fires to keep out
The cold.

Eat your hay, your day is done. Rest, old Bess,
You're home and dry, but it's bitter and cold.
Add some more straw to keep the ice from the
Stable floor.

Morning did come, bitter and cold. Old Bess
Was harnessed for a two-ton cart, forty bags
Of anthracite coal that old Bess must pull
Over hill and dale.

Over the brow of Dollis Hill, a two-ton load
A daunting task, up the hill of ice like shining
Glass, the driver led old Bess by the halter
With skid-pans on the back wheels to stop the
Cart from rolling back.

But halfway up this blessed hill, steam came
From her coat. Old Bess collapsed upon the road.

Her heart had burst with this great big load.
We heard the driver plead with her, as tears of grief
Rolled from his eyes, as he cradled her head, until
She died.

They picked her up without finesse, carving her up
For the horsemeat shop, selling her remains as
Edible flesh, as meat was scarce in wartime London.
Not many would know they'd eaten Old Bess.

Old Don

No wind farms on our cabbage patch,
The Langford Nimbys cry out in woe.
They petition the council to make this so.

Then Don Quixote is raised from the dead
To tilt at windmills on his skinny old horse
But it tossed old Don when a carrot he's fed.

Eating all the food in that cabbage patch
Don Quixote's horse became so very fat.
Standing there with lance and sword in hand
Old Don was helpless to save Langford's land.

So round and round the windmills turn
As the Nimbys retreat to hide their pride
On the day Don Quixote once more died.

So the village of Langford has ten wind
Generators and only the farmer is the
Winner as he laughs all the way to the
Bank.

Old Nick's Cooking Pot

To all my creditors
Whom I owe vast
Sums of loot:

You can have your cash,
Your pot of honey
With crippling interest,
High-yield stash.

Just follow my instructions
For the quickest route
To get every last dime
Of your high-interest loot.

Take the highway
Down Satan's Way.
Look for treble six
On the devil's door.
Knock, just once.
A warm welcome
Will be assured.

You can count your loot
By a warm fire's glow.
Spend it, burn it,
All that you've got
For you're not leaving
Old Nick's cooking pot.

Old Tom

A bolt of ragged lightning
Came crashing down.
It struck old mad Tom,
The village fool, the local clown.

Tom lit up like a neon sign.
Steam and fire came from his head
But Old Tom was far from dead.

As the smoke and ash cleared away
The village folk could hear Tom say,
'By the gods, I needed that.
'Einstein move over, Old Tom is back.'

He plugged himself into the Internet,
Draining all known knowledge from it.
Now Old Tom the village fool
Is the lord and master over all.

He built a palace in the sky,
Passing down his wisdom
To you and me.

The moral of this story is
Never go out in a thunderstorm
Because you could end up a billionaire!

On Reflection

On reflection as I cast my mind back,
Life in my youth was no bed of roses.
In fact one could say we were dirt poor.
'Twas a time in our history, a time of war,

When for five years warfare took its toll
On the nation, its people, its very soul.
But was it worth it? As I look around today
I fear this is a nation of feeble, greedy people
Who care little for the sacrifices others gave.
The cup of kindness is seen as being soft.
Hard-faced, the stuff you jack, spin on this –
Is the norm for this materialistic country?

Who gives a tom-tit any more about our soldiers?
They and their kids go hungry to keep you safe in
Rat-infested houses from Victorian times –
And who gives a Donald Duck about the dead?

Coming home in body bags, buried without honour.
Yes, on reflection I am glad I was born dirt poor
And suffered along with millions in those dark days.
We found the meaning of many words lacking today:
Compassion for others and comradeship on a scale
That will never be seen in this selfish land of Britain.
'Tis a sad reflection I bring to these pages, my friends,
But the human beings of yesteryear would shout out,
'Stop, you greedy bastards. Think of others for once.'

Once Upon a Time

Once upon a time
In the land of make-believe
Lived two wicked, evil, old men
Who always lied and deceived.

Egotistic, vain, pluralistic twits,
Cunning wizards, with evil tricks,

They told this world, 'Our word is true.
On no account would we lie to you.'
One was called Satan T Blair
Who sold his soul to the highest bid,
'Texas tea' Bush, the oil billionaire.

Now 'Texas tea' Bush and Satan T
Conjured up a war for you and me.
'I'll make you rich,' Texas T said.
'Who gives a toss
For those wounded or dead?
Let's grab that oil beneath those sands.'

They cast a spell with big dollar bills
And greedy men followed like imbeciles.
Their quest for oil came unstuck
As blood and guts gushed from the ground
A civil war is all they found.

One Ton Twelve and a Score

Who are these one ton twelve and a score
That have sat in Westminster ten years or more?
What have they done for the likes of you and me
Besides feathering their own nests so splendidly,
And the twenty that sit much higher than that,
Whilst the great bulk of us look on
At ermine robes and all that crap?

Was Clause Four a joke to these union MPs?
Did our forefathers fight to abolish this peerage crap?
Or is it just a case of 'Stuff you lot. I'm alright, Jack.'
Take note, my well-heeled trade union friends,
Your money pie, your gravy train is at its end.

Ask your dad, Mr Hilary Benn, the real
meaning of socialism
To the working class and the battle he had
To rid his titled past. The things he did for you, his kid,
So you might sit on that green leather seat
To do sweet FA for the old and the weak.

Ask John Prescott if he can sleep at night,
This working-class hero from the city of Hull.
He sold our council houses for the cheapest bid
To housing associations and wide-boy spivs.
Ten grand a plot was the average they paid,
Millionaires by the bucket this deal made.

Most of you are a mystery to me,
Never spoken and never seen,
Union MPs with more in the Lords.

Oracle

As the Earth sped onwards
Towards the dying red sun
At ever-increasing speed,

All life forms
On this once beautiful planet
Perished in the flames of hellfire.

The human race dug deep
Into Mother Earth
In a futile attempt to avoid the flames

But even those who fled
Into the deepest caves
Were winkled out by volcanic lava.

As the human race witnessed
Spontaneous combustion
Of their own bodies,

One lone mocking voice
Could be heard above all others
In the final Armageddon –
'I told you all, didn't I?',

Sneered the great Oracle of Wisdom,
'But not one of you listened.
Buy a ruddy good walk-in refrigerator.'
He laughed out loud

As he tucked into his roast-beef dinner for one.

Oskar Schindler

Throw the babies in the furnace
Of death even as they scream
Because they are not dead.

Save all you can, Oskar the brave,
Save what you can from the
Concentration camps' graves.

You lied and cheated to save all
You could from the horrors of
Germany and the great master race,
So the name of Schindler is in
History's highest place.

To Oskar.

Our Little Son

This was a poem I wrote some thirty years ago for my only child, Marc. As a little boy he was and still is our most precious gift, plus my three grandchildren.

Little son, our little son, loved so dearly by me and
Mum.

The joy you bring each day you wake from morning
Sunshine till night time's wake.

Little boy with your impish ways, brightens up our
Dullest days.

Books and soldiers on the floor, you make us smile with
Your imaginary wars.

Goodies left, baddies right, getting ready for a terrific
Fight.

End it all with one big roar, with books and soldiers in
One big heap for that final battle that will have to
Keep.

A crazy Indian you will be, chasing young Flossy
around
A tree. Little dog has had enough and runs indoors with
Huff and puff.

'Ask your mum. I don't know,' when homework starts
By the fireside glow.

The sun's gone down, it's getting late, your maths books
Will have to wait.

Brush your teeth and comb your hair, it's time for you to
Climb those stairs.

It's in your bed, tucked up warm, Mum and Dad will say
This prayer:

You precious gift, our little son, loved so dearly by
Me and Mum.

Time will fly and time will pass but our love for
You will last and last.

God bless you, Son, and keep you safe, till morning comes
And you awake.

Our Pockets Are Empty

Our pockets are empty
And we are frozen to the core.
Heating and lighting,
We can't use that anymore.

Our bellies are empty
As food bills rise to the sky.
Do we freeze or starve to death
Until this ruddy nation dies?

Insulate your bodies
With fibreglass from your lofts.
Careful how you use it.
It can make you ruddy cough.

Sleeping bags are hard to find,
Pensioners grabbed the lot –
Keeps them warm in winter.
This government don't give a tot.

We have no money to spend on you,
This government has made that plain.
Go warm yourself in supermarkets
Whilst gazing at the food.
Beg and plead with these giants
As they throw the scraps at you.

Well done, New Labour.
You've thrown the crown away

You never had a principle
To call your very own.

You find them in the dustbins
Around MPs' second homes

Our Secret Woods

'Tis a part of a wood
That Emma really knows,
With wild bush and tall trees
Wherever we may roam,

Smelling of fruiting pine trees
That reach up to the sky,
With squawking crows
As they rebuild their nests
In the high canopy of the elms,
The trees they love the best.

The echo of a barking dog
In yon distant parts –
Young Emma is a-chasing
A tree rat or a vixen or a fox.

Bright sunlight flickers
Through the trees as they sway,
Highlighting a carpet of bluebells
Hiding in this secret wood
Down my very way.

As I sit here on a fallen tree
To ponder all in nature that is good,
My little beagle bitch, Emma,
Comes a-flying from our woods.

'Twas a fox she found.
I can smell it on her coat.
The little so-and-so rolls in poo
And thinks it's all a ruddy joke.

Paradise

For the life of me I don't understand how I came to write this snippet.

Paradise is in the mind of the beholder
For one man's paradise is another's hell;
But the paradise in-between is ours to
SQUANDER.
Grasp it with both hands
For this is not a dress rehearsal –
This IS the real thing –
For you will not come this way again.

Parallel Worlds

Deep in stellar space and time
Dwells a planet like yours and mine,
A carbon copy of everything we see
With a moon and a sun that seeds.
A mirror image since time began,
They have a world that's lush and green
With all known beasts we've ever seen.

They've progressed far in this other place
With intelligence far beyond the human race.
There is no religion this far in space
For nature taught them long ago
There is no being or unseen force
We humans call almighty God.

They live as one without human greed
Unlike Earth's poor nations who beg and plead
For food and shelter for those in need.
They banished wars and violence long ago
Devoting their life to food to eat and sow.

They live in harmony with the other beasts.
They rule their planet with love and peace.
Their peoples have travelled near and far
Observing others to see how they are.
They cried out loud as they left planet Earth,
Witnessing the death of this green little place
And their brothers and sisters in a parallel space.

Pensioners Are Praying

Pensioners are praying
It stays nice and hot
For bills they're getting
Are killing quite a lot.

The gasman is greedy
As he waves his big stick.
Pay up, you old cretins,
Or I'll throw you in nick.

The electric man
Is a live wire
As he pulls every plug
You have in your house,
As he threatens to evict you
If you don't pay the bill,
Regardless of age
Or critically ill.

But where is
This government
Whilst this rape
Is going on?
Sitting on beaches
Getting a body tan
As the utilities run riot
To jack up the bills,
Bankrupting the people of
The nation that they serve –
Fat profits and payoffs
For fat corporate nerds.

Perdition's Sons

Come, you greedy
Dollar thieves,
Tell the world
How you deceived.

You sold your souls
To the dollar bill
Hand in hand
With Capitol Hill.

Giving out loans
On this and that,
Duping the unsuspecting
Into the housing trap.

Knowing full well they've
Not a chance in hell
Of ever paying it back
For the Bank of Perdition
Would see to that.

'They' made a fortune
From trust, deceived
The banks on Wall Street
Of the devil's league.

'They' made a killing
And Main Street poor are
Plunging America
To recession's front door.

Now, hunt them down,
Every last one,
Bankers of America
Perdition's sons.

Take their wealth,
Every last dime,
Throw them in jail
For a very long time.

Brand their foreheads
With a tattoo sign:
'I stole from my people,
The foulest of crimes.'

Peter's World

In the winter month of March
One bleak and frost-filled day,
A child was born late that night –
Peter, they called his name.

His mother was a hard-faced bitch,
The father was much the same,
Caring little after their carnal sex
For the little ones that came their way.

Just one of a million of unwanted kids
Fighting for a life he had never seen,
Held forever in check by cruel depravity.

The chain was broke long ago
When Peter made his break
Away from a parent and siblings,
Ones who showed him naught
But hate.

Now he is in his twilight stage,
His memory dimmed by time.
He remembers his wicked mum,
Her unbridled ferocious treatment
Of this little child called Peter,
The one she loved to hate.

Please, Mr Santa

Please, Mr Santa,
Daddy is fighting a war
The reasons for 'why'
I'm not really sure!

My daddy's been sent
To strange foreign shores
Where Christmas is alien.
Goodwill is no more.

Please wrap him in paper
And tie him with string,
Post him by airmail
To those who love him.

If you can't find my daddy
In the vast desert sands,
Redirect my letter
To Cameron's evil hands.

Perhaps he and his government
Who roam around free
Will remember the pain
They caused my mummy and me.

Political Abuse
(The Conservative Party)

When a political party
Shows contempt
For the entire nation
It should represent,
Dragging the nation
Into pigswill and dirt,
Blaming poor folk for
Misdeeds they create,
Millions suffer from
The savaging of the
Welfare state.

When a political party
Can't give a toss, the mandate
Of their party gets buried
And lost.

When they tell blatant lies
To deceive, turning to scoundrels
Of elected thieves, donning the
Mantle of the far-off right,
These are the times we
Britons must fight.

'They' want you in chains,
A slave to their whims
When only the rich
And powerful will win.

They've become fascists,
The far-right scum –
Nazi dictators of the
Upper-class ones.

The time has come
For all of us to shout,
'Enough is enough.
Leave this Parliament
Whilst you can
Or you'll get battered
To death by avenging
Hands.'

Press-Ganged

Did they ever give a shit
If they lived or died?
They couldn't vote till twenty-one.
Press-ganged into khaki suits,
State murder, the end for some...

The establishment,
The monarch, the dross,
Leeching, preaching,
Blue-blooded pricks –
The scum of Britain
These spineless gits...

This worthless tripe
Of the upper crust
Imprisoned young men
For a two-year stay
As cannon fodder
For empire wars,
Expendable lads of
National Service days...

No human rights
Or sparse dignity –
A mule to kick,
The beast of prey.
Some young lads
Died for these gits
Blue-blooded
Fucking inbred idiots...

Palestine, the Jewish war,
NS boys died by the score.
In Malaya's jungles of death
Voteless young men perished.
From Kenya and Cyprus
To the hot Arab states,
NS boys gave up their life
To feed that sick dream,
The status quo for
Empire and Queen...

In Aden and Suez
The NS have fought,
Spilt their blood
In faraway wars,
Expendable life
On foreign shores.
The Falklands
Was the Maggot's war –
All regular soldiers
For National Service
Is no more...

But never-ending
Is the need for blood:
The Gulf, One and Two,
The Balkans, have
Taken our brave lads
So blue bloods can keep
The life that they have
For black gold,

Or Texas tea.
The wealth of others
These arseholes do thieve...

Yes, I could die in Cyprus fighting EOKA
But I could not vote. How fucking sick is that?

Proud of English Village Names

I went to Shitterton
The other day
But landed in Crapstone,
A village far away.

You'd feel a fool,
Said the man fromTwatt.
Nob End and Pidley
Are just as bad as that.

Thong is Ugly so is Pratt's Bottom
But as good as Muff.
But Upper Dicker
Is near Ball's Green
And Bell End.

So Cockmouth
And Spital in the Street
Must be near Lickey End.

'Tis the truth. These are some of our village names.

Public Servants

Just got my new council rate demand. Made me feel quite sick when I looked at what I was paying for (and not getting) plus the turds who run our council want a raise!

Who are they,
These servile creeps?
Just public servants
Who fleece
The pockets of everyone
Then pay themselves
A king's ransom.

Sitting in judgment
Of you and me,
Deciding how much tax
They can thieve
And what lies to tell
So they can deceive.

They've forgotten
Who they are.
Just public servants
Who do OUR BID.
Our very wish
Is our command.

But not one of them
Would understand
We pay tax

That gives them a job,
Then they rip us off,

The council yobs.

Radio Days

'Twas forces' favourites
From way back in '47 –
Jean Metcalfe,
This Scots lass,
The forces' choice
With this wonderful
Dreamy voice.
'With a song
In my heart' was
The signature tune
Played to millions
On a Sunday
Afternoons.

*I found the music to this song and it brought tears
to my eyes, for I was a serving soldier
In Cyprus and for nearly two years lived under
canvas back in 1955. Jean Metcalfe
And Cliff Michelmore hosted* Forces Favourites
*on a Sunday afternoon and played the songs
That the wives and girlfriends had requested
for their loved one serving in the British forces.
In those moments I witnessed many a grown
man with tears rolling down his face.*

Radio Heart-Beat

Hi, folks, I was just tuning my crystal set and my 'cats-whisker' found this super radio channel.

Radio Heart-Beat is on the air
Pumping out love to the atmosphere.
Tune in your radio to two five nine,
A channel of love and passion sublime.

Turn up the volume so others might hear
The music of love and carnal delights.
On long and passionate steamy hot nights
Radio Heart-Beat is waiting for you.
Just push in a button or turn on a knob
For hours of passion, love and romance,
An elixir of love to make your heart throb.

Reality Dreams

There is a journey
We all must make
When our time on this planet
We forsake.

This is the beginning
Of a fantastic dream
With your soul and mind
Released at last
As you start on a journey
To the future or your past.

Released from the body
That created your mind
You can wander the Universe
Till the end of time.

You're just a link
In the order of things
For your mind is connected
To our final dream.
Truth is reality;
Your mind is set free.

To travel in time,
To live that wild dream,
Sit on a moonbeam
To ride its pure light
To travel to galaxies
Far out of sight.

Wander and ponder
In the heart of a sun.
Soak up the knowledge
Of how it began.
Catch a lift
On a shooting star.
Travel the cosmos
Both near or so far.

Go to the nebula,
Blackholes of time.
Thoughts are not altered
In a vortex that crushes
A planetary system
Down to fine dust.

Walk in dimensions
Way out of your own.
Visit new beings
From galaxies afar.
Watch them progress
As they reach for the stars.

Your future is endless,
Just you wait and see.
When you start on
YOUR journey
Of reality dreams.

Revolution

Never in my 77 years on this godforsaken earth have
I witnessed a government turn on its own people so
Brutally and never have I witnessed the callousness
And single-minded pursuit of driving a group of British
Working-class people to the doors of Victorian
workhouses.

The script for this three-year horror
story of persecution
And deprivation of this group of
hard-working families
Could have been written by Paul Joseph
Goebbels who
Was a German politician and
Reich Minister of Propaganda
In Nazi Germany from 1933 to 1945,
and one of Adolf Hitler's
Closest friends.

The hated Coalition government
of Conservative and Liberal
Democrat MPs will go down in
the annals of British history
As one of infamy and sheer hatred
of a group of British citizens
That in our recent history has never
been seen in living memory.

The words of lying, cheating two-faced
underhanded cretins is
A mild description of what was called
the Tory party some
Years ago and a new title that emulated
from the dictators of
South America now hangs around the necks
of most Con-Dem MPs and the word
Junta fits them well, but unlike the military
juntas of South America
This junta has used the right-wing media
such as newspapers, the BBC and the
Royal family to wage war on the
working class of Britain.

The Labour Party is just as guilty of
lack of support for their
Core supporters and for four long years
Miliband contemplated
His navel and said nothing as the Con-Dems
hacked the working class to pieces.

In an orgy of destruction of the welfare state
that even Himmler
Would be proud of, and one speech that
promises 'jam tomorrow' in regards
To energy bills, does not make a real socialist.

There are 650 reasons why the mass
of the British people
Must rise up in revolution and the reason
is the calibre and

Honesty of our Members of Parliament,
none bar a few live up
To the yardstick of a 1945 politician
because most of today's
Intake should have their hands chopped
off for stealing money
From the public purse dressed in the
guise of 'expenses'.

Injustice is rife at the bottom of the
pile and the working class
Are being used by the 'Houses of
Crime and Corruption' as
The sacrificial lambs that are paying
for the misdeeds of the
City of London and the vile crooks
and robbers who stalk these
Tall buildings of the gods of gold and oil.

This junta must go and go quickly to
save what's left of their
Dignity and morality and most
of all to stop unnecessary
Bloodshed that was witnessed in the
poll tax riots in the
Days of another Tory fascist called
Thatcher but this time the
Whole nation will rise up and demand
that they go and if the
Queen quibbles over royal protocol,
then let her be the last

One to sit in judgement of the
masses as we vote for a
Republic of the British Homelands
and the House of Windsor
Can vanish into the realms of history.

Rich Man, Poor Man

The poor man sighed,
Is this what they mean?
By the gods' will,
Can't he see all
These mouths to fill?

The politician's son
Grew strong and fair,
Boasting great wealth
Of a multimillionaire.

A motto for him:
Make others your slaves.
Live life to the full;
It could end any day.

His wealth brought titles,
A massive living space.
It brought him a wife
With a sweet angelic face.

They travelled so far
All over this world
But something was missing
From his heart of stone –
The love of a human.
He was terribly alone.

He spurned his wife
And distrusted his god –
His life was meaningless.

Gold was but candy floss.

The poor man worked
In dirt and the factory's oil.
He married for love
The girl of his dreams.
Their needs were simple,
The very basic of needs.

This lightened his load
Down life's high road
For love was their strength
As through the ages they went.
They lived out their days
With a life that's well spent.

Now, he died with a smile
Cast over his lips and a look
Of hope shone within his eyes.
For after all when said and done
Who was the richest of both these
Sons?

River of Ink

Give me a pencil
Or a pen.
Give me paper
To go with them.

Give me sadness,
Give me joy,
Give love to me
In verse or song
With pen to paper
I will do no wrong.

Give me poetry
That speaks the truth.
Make it rhyme
In simple words
Not in a vocabulary
Those nobody's heard.

Give me life
In all its forms.
Make it simple
For all to read,
Not confused
In a jumbled phrase
That leaves the reader
In an utter daze.

With pen to paper
Speak your mind.
Search your soul
To its innermost depths.
Write it down
And see what you get.

Don't be afraid
If you think it's not right.
Remember the pen
Is more powerful
Than Excalibur's smite.

Keep it flowing,
Your river of ink,
Then post it to the world
And see what they think.

Maggie & Ron

They say that Maggie had a crush on Ron and he had the devil's job to control his massive giant hard-ons whenever the Cast-Iron Lady came to stay and Mrs R was far away.

Beanpole Ron they called him then for like a tentpole in his pants he would flash it at Maggie at every chance.
Ron loved her strict iron will and the whip she lashed on his bum when he would shout, 'No, no, Maggie, you will make me cum.'

'Twas mutual love at first bite which gave Mrs T such delight. There she was dressed in black, her leather suit and kneehigh boots on Ron's bare back as she smacked his bum with terrific force, but old Ron loved it like hot chilli sauce.

Who cares if the world is blown to bits as Ron fondles Maggie's cast-iron tits as she bites and tongues a tentpole dick? 'What about Russia?,' his aides all say. 'Fuck them all,' Old Ron said. 'I've got the Maggot in my bed. I will fuck them all, another day.'

Ronald Reagan and the Maggot

He was a third-rate actor who had a big gob who undermined America and thought he was a god.

The politics of greed, a Republican clown who became the President, a dictatorial fool whose jokes were not very funny at all.

As right-wing as they come, this man was deranged and admired the Maggot on the British political stage.

Thatcher the Snatcher was evil enshrined, for like little Ronnie, as the sun shone from his arse, they were as one in the political class.

The Maggot destroyed all that she touched – no such thing as society. She preached and she preened, so Ronald just copied her vile wicked dreams.

They changed this world to a planet full of hate for the wealth in the pocket is the ones who dictate.

So remember these two, who we thought were in love, for they were not as gentle as turtle doves. Greed was their god, their Valhalla on high, that left us all eating the crumbs from their pie.

Round and Round

Wait a minute, I've been here before
When the housing market crashed to the floor.
Up it went in a crazy housing boom
When you'd pay a million for just one room.

But down it spiralled in an almighty crash
When the banks all said, 'We are out of cash.'
So negative equity is here once more
As your house and homes crash to the floor.

Your house is worthless, just bricks and muck
But what the heck, who gives a rubber duck?
For round and round the money tree goes
I'll catch it next time the housing boom grows.

Run of the Arrow

Run you fools, the spirit warriors of the Indian
Nations are after you. Run for your life; it means
Death for you.

They flex their bows and the arrows are swift in
Flight, so run you white man, the Red Indians are
Coming after you.

They want their lands back and coyote wailing his
Lonely song that never ends and the howl of the
Wolf packs as the night-times descend.

The hunting grounds of prairies wild and the
Buffalo herds that covered this land from coast to
Coast, their hooves are heard.

So the tribes of the American plains aim their
Arrows high to the heavens above to drive out the
White man from the lands they love.

Leave now, before the arrows fall and impale the
White man and his greed and turn them into
Tumbleweed.

So it is said by the spirit gods, as the run of the
Arrow is not an ancient dream of a prophecy in
Waiting that all white man will see...Noble Tribes of
America.

Sackcloth and Ashes

Did you know that starting a charity is the quickest way to make your fortune? If you took the time to look at the published accounts of the big charities in the UK, you would be shocked at the salaries some give themselves (plus perks). My idea for this poem came from the film Tom Thumb *which starred the late Terry-Thomas and Peter Sellers as two crooks who stole the from the local bank and came to blows as they tried to cheat each other when dividing the loot!*

Sackcloth and ashes
Above reproach,
Is the public perception
All charities hope!

Many a billion
Have gone their way
Spending 'your' money
In a simple way.

It's 'one for them'
And 'two for me'
When dishing out
Your charity.

They pay themselves
A fabulous sum,
A king's ransom
For everyone.

The millions you give
Are in their bank
Earning vast interest
From which they take.

'One for them'
And 'two for me'

As they give 'your' money
To those in need.

Satan's Priestess (Sarah Palin)

Sorcerer of Arctic snows,
Death and destruction
Your evil does sow.

The pure white Arctic
Is stained bright red.
Animals are butchered,
Sacrifices to Satan
His priestess has bled.

The devil in black,
Or Texas tea –
Crude oil
To you and me.

Drill and kill,
The call of the wild.
Slaughter the whales,
The great polar bear,
Satan's priestess
Just could not care.

Bribe all the natives
With mountains of cash.
Dig up their homeland
With open-cast mines,
Destroying the environment –
Gone forever
Till the end of time.

The devil is Shell.

With BP drilling crews
Who pay the priestess
For Satan's deeds
As the top of the world
Just slowly bleeds.

Self-Importance

The best thing since sliced bread,
This astounding knowledge in my head
For I am the best at what I do.
The system would fail if not for you.

I'm the biggest cog in the wheel
Which keeps it turning without a spill.
They flatter and praise all you do –
Their very existence is down to you.

I strut around just like a king.
I'm so important to everything.
Then it ended with a 'chip'.
They stuck my knowledge on a 'byte'.
A computer took my job overnight.

My self-importance is no more
As the smiling boss showed me the door.
My world had ended with a thump
When 'chips' for brains they did dump.

Sell

Sitting back in my old rocking chair, I cast my mind's eye around this sorry old world of ours – the calibre of our world's leaders came into mind. In my days we had real men as leaders of this world, Eisenhower, Churchill to name but two. But then I look at what we have today, Bush and Blair (say no more) and I wondered how they came to be at the top of the pile. This is how I think it happened:

Sell your mother, to make a buck.
Sell your granny to the garbage truck.
Sell your soul, your wife and kids,
Sell them all to the highest bid.
Sell corruption, arms and death.
Sell your country, you are pledged.
Sell your mind to religious freaks.
Sell them hatred, intolerance and grief.
Sell us all, the whole ruddy lot.
Sell humanity to the melting pot.
When it melts, just skim the top,
Bush and Blair are what we got.
Stop the world, I want out of here.

Shallow

It's a sick little word
Describing the nature
Of a cyberspace
Where people
Can wear two
Kinds of face.

A 'surface friend'
Who never was,
A-leeching and preaching,
Warning and scorning,
Sorrowful soul
Who milks you dry
To reach a goal.

Gone up the ladder
In the social class –
Millionaire hubby
Out of my league.
Still one of the lads
They would have
You believe.

Cast-off friend
Your days are done.
They must culture
More poets,
The upper-crust ones,
But most are shallow

And have the same dream:
Getting to the top
Of the social cream.

But once up the top
It's a long way to fall.
Your poems and friends
Mean nothing at all.
'He is my hand,'
A true friend would say,
But that is not possible
You threw them away.

Stuff the fcuking lot.

Shame on You, America

It's shame on America, the land of the free,
when you preach
Goodness and mercy to the faces of your
poor and then deny them
Medicines that shut out death's door.

Shame on your doctors who couldn't care
less as your fellow
Americans and your own kith and kin
have to eat catmeat to
Pay YOU your bill for a dime's worth of
medicines in green dollar bills.

Shame on you repugnant folks in the
South who shout out the
Loudest about the religion of greed
with your hands in THEIR
Pockets you pillage and thieve the
last vestige of kindness you
Left in the trough when you shout
at your kinsmen, 'Just fuck off and rot.'

Shame on you Americans who turn
a deaf ear to crying and
Pleading of the millions of your poor sanctimonious
Republicans, the harbours of greed.
Open your fat wallets and
Start feeding the millions in need.

Shame on the man who brought this
about who sat in the
White House at his plush Oval Office desk,
whilst 'they' ripped up
America and sold it as scrap to his
chums in the Senate who
Called him a fine chap.

But where are the religious,
the pious church ones who
Preach from the scriptures about
the mercy of kings then turn a
Blind eye at the plight of the poor?
Who cross over the road to
Dismiss and ignore.

So shame on you, America, as the
rest of the world watch your
Great nation decline from the top of the tree,
the leader of men
In a great democracy to the seething
and greedy collectors of
Wealth whose main aim in life is to
abandon the notion of the
Concept of FREE HEALTH.

Shame on You, God

Shame on you God, you Stone Age freak.
How many more must die
Before your blood lust is complete?

You had the blood of six million Jews.
'Yahweh,' they cried,
As they went to their deaths.
As the doors of the ovens
Slammed shut on their screams
God just sat there
Not doing a blind thing.

Shame on you God, you Stone Age freak.
How many more must die
Before your blood lust is complete?

Pol Pot, another creature of God's evil ways:
His Khmer Rouge took Cambodia
Back to year one in the human age,
Slaughtered the innocent, a million bar one
But God never intervened
To save his Cambodian sons.

Shame on you God, you Stone Age freak.
How many more must die
Before your blood lust is complete?

The horror of Vietnam and four million dead:
Fifty-six thousand American soldiers

Are buried in strange foreign soil
As their leaders plan more massacres
In the name of Gulf Oil.

Shame on you God, you Stone Age freak.
How many more must die
Before your blood lust is complete?

Dafur and Rwanda where genocide raged:
The children of God are slaughtered
And maimed and cry out to the God
Each one of them seeks
As he bellows down from heaven,
'Turn the other cheek.'

God is not real; he lives in your minds –
A mind-control trick of biblical times.
Switch off the circuit that's making you blind.
Look for the evil, the monstrous humankind.
Their motive for death is pure human greed
As they conjure up a god so you are deceived.

Shame on you humans, you mind-control freaks.
Tell them the truth, it's your wealth that you seek.
The spilling of blood means nothing to you.
Just tell them it's God's will, you sick human freak.

Sharks and Spivs

The golden square of
Dick Whittington thieves,
Pinstriped cowboys
Who rip us off,
Underselling shares
Then buying them back,
Dipping their fingers
Into other's cash.
Stockmarkets crumble
By the monies they've grabbed.

Sharks and spivs,
London's trash,
A leftover from the '40s
When 'barrow boys' were flash.
The wide boys of Canary Wharf
Who would flog their grannies,
Their mums and dads,
Throw in their sisters,
For a handful of cash.

Money is their god,
All power to some,
The scum of this earth.
Prosecute the cow sons

Sister Rita

That fatal day so long ago,
The sister so loved,
So dearly missed,
Perished with husband
Along with her kids.

How I miss our sisterly chats
Of life today and this and that.
The dearest friend that ever could be
If ever trouble threatened my family.

The truest friend that graced this earth.
The wonderful moments you left behind,
Sweetness and kindness the tender times.

A wonderful mother and faithful wife,
My sister Rita lived every moment
Of her sweet and tender life.

Full of fun when we were together,
Laugh and giggle as sisters do.
The silly things that made us laugh
Like getting the kids to take a bath.
The good-looking men who made a pass;
These innocent times made us laugh.

Always beautiful but never vain,
We prided ourselves on being the same,
Never jealous of the other's lot.
Her precious memory is not forgot.

Sitting at the Crossroads

Down the road to nowhere,
Up the hills of shame and
Cross the path of fruitless blame
Then pass the buck again.

Sitting at the crossroads
As history passes by
Will never solve the horror of
Why African children have to die.

Carve a road that's straight and true,
Create it in our hearts and minds,
Carve the road to Africa
Before the starvation starts!

Sitting on the Fence

Beware of splinters,
The tiny little
Niggardly ones
Piercing your skin
Into your bum.

But sitting and waiting
To see if you fall
Is the nastiest
Splinter of them all.

'Here are some tweezers,'
A true friend would say
As they warn all others
Who sit on this fence.
The splinters on here
Are as sharp
As your tongue.
Sit still, do nothing,
Before you're the
Next one.

Skid Row

In every city and every town
There are some places out of bounds.
Down Hard Luck Street and Beggars Row,
My friends, this really is not the place to go.

You're on the slippery slope to nowhere
And sliding forever deep, falling ever quicker
Until Skid Row you'll surely meet.

You're bottom of the pecking pile,
the dross of humankind.
The life of wealth and comfort,
you left them far behind.
Drinking meths and cider brews,
an early death is for you.
Now Skid Row will always welcome you,
the powerful and
The weak.

If by chance you cross Hard Times Way,
without the help you seek,
Skid Row is unforgiving and
will make you pay the costs.
Your wife and kids, your dog, your home,
In Skid Row all you had is LOST.

Sleepwalking

Beware, my friends,
The phone on which you speak,
The mobile you do text,
Landline sending fax,
Spies are after that.

From this moment on
Your life to the state belongs.
Everything you utter,
Every sound you make,
Will go onto a computer
Belonging to the state.

Quangos will use it
To push you to the wall,
Pointing at some garbage
You never said at all.

Take care of every
Sound you make.
Whisper if you can.
Big Brother is really here.
He is waiting in that van.

Your freedom went
This darkest day –
Just open up your eyes.

You're sleepwalking
Into deadly danger
Of a nation of little spies.

Snobs

There are two types of snob in this human world, the monetary and the intellectual. Both look down on those who are neither.

'I pay my char the lowest rate,'
Bragged the British snob
To the wealthy Yank.
'So do we,' said the snob
From the US of A.
'But in olden days
They called them slaves.'
'My one is as thick
As a household brick,'
Sniggered the posh,
Snobby British bitch.
'You make me laugh,'
Said the Yank from the
Upper middle class.
'For a dollar more,
It will kiss my arse.'
This type of snob
Made their stack
Just by laying
On their backs
But the ones to detest
Most of all
Are the cretins who
Take us all for fools.
They talk down to us

And pat our heads,
Looking at you
As though you're dead.

Sneering at your
Mother tongue,
They are the worst
Of the snobby ones.

Snowdrops

The harshness of winter's soil,
No light, no sun, the dried-out
Leaves of bygone years but life
Does move and starts to sprout
When the heads of snowdrops
All jump out.

Pushing and shoving with olive-
Green leaves, covering the forest
In carpets of white, snowdrops
Of winter, a cold day's delight.

Solitude

Alone at night by a glowing log fire,
Bright embers are flickering.
Strange dreams they inspire.

You slump in your armchair
As you ponder your lot.
The stillness is echoed
By the chimes of a clock.

It's two in the morning,
Just you and your dog
Asleep by the fireside
As you add a new log.

A puffing of steam,
Bright yellow flames,
It's crackling and spitting,
Yellow brightness again.

The shadows are dancing
Around things short and tall,
Painting strange pictures
On ceilings and walls.

This time is your own,
No dragons to slay.
This solitude you crave for
Many others invade.

These moments are precious,
Your own space and time.

A solitude of silence
Of times which are mine.

Spare a Copper

'Spare a copper
For the blind man's eye,'
Whispers a beggar
As you hurry on by.

His clothing is ragged
And seen better days,
A face that's haggard
And needing a shave.

'Spare a copper
For the blind man's eye,'
He whispers again
As you stop near by.

You notice the scars
That cover his face
And notice the eyes
That stare into space.

Then you notice the medals
Brilliant and clean
Plus all the ribbons
Of the service he's seen.

Most are for the cold
Of the Baltic States.
You ask him a question,
'What happened, old mate?'

I was a soldier of
Country and Queen
Fighting your wars
To keep you all free.

I was blown up in ambush
In Southern Iraq that
Killed all my buddies
In that terrible attack.

Blew out my eyes,
A soldier no more,
And this is my reward,
Homeless and poor.

I gave him some money,
All that I had.
Is this the way to
Treat our brave lads?

'Spare a copper
For the blind man's eye,'
I heard him pleading
As I walked on by.

*As an ex-serviceman, I find the MoD One of the
most callous and despotic arms of government.
They just don't give a toss for our veterans.*

Spineless

I've opened a shop
Called
Backbones and Minds
To replace the spine
Most have lost.
To free their minds
Others do keep
Removing the gags
So they may speak.

'Tis a slippery road
You lot do slide
As right-wing prigs
Censor your views,
Threaten expulsion
To the emboldened few.
Say, 'Stuff you lot,
Don't give me that crap.
Millions have died
To put paid to that.'

So come with me
As I open my shop,
As I dish out
Minds and backbones
So you can fight
The sinister censors
Who prowl these sites.

Stairway to the Stars

Just build yourself a ladder
Ten billion steps or more.
Prop it up against a fluffy cloud
Anchored to the earthly floor.

Take a step, one by one,
As you slowly reach the top,
Passing up more ladders
The millions you all forgot.

The stairway is completed
As we climb upon a star
To travel to the galaxies
So close and so very far.

Keep on building your exit,
Your stairway to the stars,
The ladder to the Milky Way
To salvation both near and far.

Don't look down – way up far
This earth cannot be seen.
It's clouded in corruption
The worst the earth has ever been.

Let the meek go first
Upon these steps.
The rich can go on last.
As we pull away the ladders
Now they can kiss
OUR fucking arse.

Stardust

We are but stardust, you and me.
We came from a place called eternity.

Once there was nothing in the void of time,
Just stardust and gases, water and slime.

We came from space light years ago
From a stellar big bang and the sun's afterglow.

A chemical soup of a thousand and one
In just the right place from the heat of our sun.

This stardust was cooked in a big ball of stew,
Just the right ingredients to create me and you.

A fireball of stardust is earth's distant fate
On a journey to immortality we once more make.

For if you took the time to think
Our life is but a meteorite streak.

Sticks and Stones

Sticks and stones may break your bones
But names will sometimes hurt you.

Some words will cut and fester
And not wither on the vine.

A chance remark or silly joke
Can cut and sting like angry bees
When driven from their hive.

Words can fester like a septic boil
But boils can heal and fade away.
Alas words can fester all your days.

So forgive the ones who said them.
Don't take them to your grave
Unlike the boil that fades away
Without a scar to see.

Words will never fade away
They stay until eternity.

Stuff All the Bankers

I say stuff 'em all,
Every last one of
The bankers and wankers
Who created this mess.
Throw them in jail,
Bury the keys,
Till they pay back the loot
They stole from me.

Ronald Biggs
Got thirty years.
Twelve in all did
The train job –
Three hundred years
Slapped up in nick
For mouldy old notes
Worth two million quid.

But the bankers and wankers
Who stole from us all
Were given a fat bonus
With millions of stock.
Have those who rule us
Got a dose of brain rot?

So I say to you all,
Take out a loan
For millions of pounds.
Spend it or hide it,

Spread it around.
If they ask for it back,

Say that you're
A wanker of a banker
From the golden square.
Bankers pay nothing
For stealing the loot.

Stuff you all,
Who gives a hoot
If MPs and barons
Are the spivs
In flash suits?
Throw them in nick.
Melt down the keys
So they can't rob us again
Whenever they please.

Wankers and bankers, who gives a hoot?

Stuff Them All On the BBC

Where are the arseholes
I thought were friends?
Gutless sewage,
The whole fucking lot.
They've made me so sick
That I've got the trots.

Queenly, my soapbox friend,
You two-faced git,
You're no friend.
You USE everyone
For your rotten ends.

You are the matriarch
Of that site,
The ruddy queen bee
With the gob to bite,
Stringing them along
And don't give a toss.
If one of them goes
It's no fucking loss.

And that other tosspot
Who slid from the mud,
Self-righteous git
Who is full of shit.
He's got it made
With his viper in tow.
'I don't like that man.
He better go.'

But beware, you fools,
He sits in his nest,
Rubbing his hands,
Saying,
'Which one is next?'
He's got it made.
You're under his thumb.
Kick him out.
He is just a twat.
That site is not his.
It brings in the adverts,
Your net passports,
To create all the biz,
But he bathes in the glory
As you kiss his fat arse
And thank him for nothing
For letting you think
He is sent from heaven
And his shit does not stink.

I am glad I went
But sad and a fool.
The people I trusted
Were gutless and cruel.
Some stood by what they said
But the majority just bowed
Their COWARDS' heads.

Stuff you all, may your pens break
When you write about truth and friendships
You forsake.

(A training poem from my days on the BBC.)

Super Grass

Our freedoms going, one by one,
We are clueless of what's gone on –

A super grass down every street,
Friends and neighbours dare not speak.

Surveillance cameras in every road,
Your civil liberties they erode.

You dare not think or talk aloud
When the thought police are around.

'They' want your genes, your DNA,
On the biggest computer of the day.

'They' want the profile of everyone
To point the finger or a gun!

There's a satellite camera in the sky
Tracking your movements until you die.

Those George Orwell days of '84
Are facts, not fiction anymore.

Wake up my friends, before it's too late,
Before we become the the Big Brother state.

It's a funny old world – George Orwell's real name
Was Eric Arthur BLAIR!

That Final Dream

Not to wake and feel the pain
To close my eyes and dream again,

Not to scream at every move
Or suffer the indignity
Of a feeding tube,

I long for peace
That sleep will bring
And that final journey
We will all begin.

My wish is now
To travel in time
And leave this sick old world
Far behind,

To spend eternity
In time and space
Far away from the human race,

To have my soul and mind intact
As I meet many more of like mind,
Travelling through galaxies
Till the end of time,

To gaze in wonderment
At what we see
When we leave our body
For that final dream.

Thatcher the Evil One

First there was Thatcher,
Or the Maggot for some,
Then Willy Whitelaw
A fat Conservative bum...

Geoffrey Howe, a soft-spoken one,
Who stabbed the Maggot when
Her time had to come...

Nigel Lawson who in 1983
Stole all our money from you and me.
He stole the 'family silver' for his
Tory chums and feathered the nest
For his City chums...

Ding dong bell, the Marylebone twit
Hailshame who made up the laws
For these despicable twits...

Plus a host of others in this terrible crew
Who lorded it over me and you:
Soames and Pym and John Biffen too
Were all part of the Thatcher
Wrecking crew...

Wakeham and MacGregor, Atkins and Young
All four were called Thatcher's chums...
Hurd and Brittan with his friend called Nott,
Along with King of the 'Nasty Lot',

The mad monk called Joseph, or the demented

Jew, all held sway over me and you, along with
Baker and Kenneth Clark, buddies of Tebbit
The Prince of the Dark...

Fowler, born in '38 to a life of luxuries he would
Never forsake, was another leech of the Thatcher years
Created a baron at the end of his career...

Mick Howard, a Jewish immigrant's son who became
Tory from his Welsh homeland, forgot his roots and
The tough working class and bent over backwards
To kiss the Maggot's arse. Baron Mick of
Lympe in the county of Kent, a turncoat of Wales
The Welsh shan't forget...

Then there was Walker and Cecil Parkinson too
Who had the hots for Thatcher for a year or two.
Heseltine was greedy for power and fame
But resigned from her government over the
Westland Helicopters fame...

Jenkins and Patten, both upper-class toffs
Who milked the system with upper-crust gobs.
Patten was governor of a Far East state
That made him baron of a county estate...

This list is not the end of the damned
And the dead who served under Thatcher,
the Maggot to some, and still can be seen
As Cameron's old chums
Who lick his Eton arse

And wipe his filthy bum
For one more taste of power
From Tory cesspit chums...

*The gift of a poet is a long memory and these scum are
burnt into my mind.*

Thatcher, the God of Greed

We all must remember why the UK is plunging into the deepest financial crisis it has ever known in its history, even deeper than the Wall Street crash of 1929.

For Britain, it started in the 1980s with the most reviled political leader this country has ever spawned, a member of a party whose philosophy has always been and always will be, 'Stuff you lot, we come first', a party of pure selfishness and ultimate greed.

The Tory Party under the leadership of the Maggot decimated our country with her sick sense of worth and greedy attitude to our nationalised industries and spectre of the City spivs rubbing their hands in glee at every sell-off of what belonged to every man, woman and child in Britain. The Maggot first made her mark in British politics when she decided that the British school children of the day should not receive free school milk, the first vile sign of her true greedy nature.

That period of time was repugnant to witness – the 'family silver' was being stolen from its rightful owners, the people of Britain, who were powerless to change the course of history.

Starting with the sale of the GPO, this galvanised the 'pig-in-the-trough' mentality of the City and the Tory Party, which grabbed and gobbled whole swathes of the 'silver' that has kept many of them and their aristocratic families in great luxury even to this very day.

At the time the Maggot was worshipped like a demagogue by all those foul creatures in the City and a great deal of her party gave praise to the greedy one. Mass unemployment was her vile tool to keep the 'other half' in their place at the bottom of the heap, typical of many party tricks she lavished on the British public.

She single-handedly ensured closure of nearly all our state-owned coal mines and alienated great masses of the British public against her but her downfall came when the greedy bitch tried and failed to bring in the hated poll tax, which caused mass riots all over Britain.

Her sell-by date had passed; her own gutless MPs were drawing straws to tell her to pack her bags and go for they knew that she had become a great liability to them winning another election that was on the horizon.

But this evil creature had done more damage to the British culture than the historians will ever admit when its time to write her obituary for she fostered the notion that greed is good and there is no such thing as society, the attitude adopted by millions of

young Britons who became known as yuppies – who are amongst the leading political tribe of the Tory Party for they have the same uncaring attitude as their mentor, the Maggot.

The scene is now set for the final phase of Thatcher, God of Greed; politics in Britain is brimful of Thatcher's children – even in the Labour Party her philosophy of 'sell everything for a fat buck' is alive and well, but now it's called PFI.

No checks and balances are in place even after the greedy banks went bust. They still worship the criterion that greed is good and until an example of rightful punishment is meted out to those who stole the world's wealth, greed will always be good.

Thatcher's Crinkle Kids

The circle of life
Is complete.
The 'shoes of age'
Are on their feet.
These yuppie people
Of a bygone age,
They've finally reached
Their twilight stage.
Don't be fooled
If they are old and grey,
They feathered
Their nests in a selfish way,
Making a fortune
By greed and stealth
By plundering
The nation of its wealth –
Gas and electric
To name but two
Owned by the many
And not this crew.
'Thatcher's Kids',
This greedy breed,
Grabbed and gobbled
Like pigs in a trough,
Destroying our 'silver',
The whole ruddy lot.
Don't pity them now
When old and grey,
They made a vast fortune

And stashed it away.
Deceitful and cunning

When quite young,
Nothing has changed
With these 'crinkly' ones.
So remember each time you pay your bills,
For gas and electric, and water too,
You're paying out dividends
To this CRINKLY OLD FEW.

The Politician, the Political Class

These unspeakable cretins
Of the political class
Worse than the detritus
From my tum
Who pillage our wealth
In vast sums,
They spend 'our' money
On personal greed,
These stinking, rotten
Diabolical thieves.
They lie and cheat,
All dirty deeds,
And these cretins
Pass laws for you and me.
Up to their necks
In sleaze and muck
Who once in power
Don't give a rubber duck.
They have no respect
For any class.
They live a life
Of pomp and wealth,
Making their 'pot'
By greed and stealth.
They are the dross
Of human kind
Not even fit
To kiss our behinds.

The Angels of the Wards

She sacked our cleaners,
The angels of the wards.
They kept them clean.
That made us safe
When hospitals
Were such a friendly place.

But Maggot Thatcher
Mucked it up (should be an F).
She sold them off
To the highest bid.
She sacrificed our safety
For a pocketful of quids.

MSRA is here and C. difficile,
Hospital bugs that really kill.
The Maggot let them in,
The 80s hero of the super rich
Who pay homage to the evil bitch,

Cutting corners and paying less
'They' have left our hospitals
In such a disgusting filthy mess.
Thousands died as government's lied.
They know the reason
Why the innocent really died.

Bring back our angels
Who also made tea.

Let them clean our hospitals
A job that they knew

And made it safe
For me and for you.

The Ballad of 'Us' and 'Them'

There is a system that rules your life – it began when you were born and will last until you die: 'Us' and 'Them' must always be, divided forever by inequality.

Born to rule, 'Them' will say, we have the wealth that makes you servants and slaves, for 'Us' and 'Them' it will always be, with 'Them' as the main priority.

You do as we say and not as we do. Remember your place as we look down on you. We will take your jobs and all you possess and give it to China to make on the cheap, then sell it to you for we know how to cheat.

We are the masters of the whole human race. Our money and wealth will keep you in check, so tape up your mouths and close down your mind and pay homage to 'Them', the superior humankind.

The Band of Gold

On her finger
I placed a band of gold,
Praying it may be there
When we grew old.

We were young
When we said our vows.
Spring was blooming
With blossom on boughs.

A band of gold
For my love divine
To carry us through
The years of time.

But looking back
Down memory lane,
We had our hopes
And lots of pain

But it brought us closer
Through all the hurt
And stormy weather
Now our hair has turned
To shades of grey.

We thank our love
That showed the way
As together we've grown old.
We praise that ring,
That band of gold.

The Beast Within

Is there a beast in everyone,
Lurking in the shadows of human ones?
No room for love in this demented beast,
Just terror and hatred you unleash,

Crushing kindness with your claws,
Ripping hearts out with your jaws.
Captive loved ones you turn to stone,
A slave to terror when you're alone.

Mental cruelty, unbridled hate,
The beast within you will create
The will to live and breathe no more
To end this torment at death's door.

But this tale I tell is true and could happen
To any of you, for this was the fate of
Someone we loved, who took this torture
For thirty years but hid away her pain
And tears to protect her flock in the early years.

The Bedford Ring

It's a fact that in this part of the UK babies were born with a ring mark around the skulls. It was passed down from the times of the lord and master days when men would doff their caps whenever the squire of the manor should pass their way. But over hundreds of years of servitude and serfdom a ring mark around his head is now a feature of all male babies' heads in Bedfordshire... now they all vote Tory.

The Bedford ring:
It's over the course of hundreds of years
The Bedford ring did first appear.
It's a sign of serfdom, of cringing twits,
of a people who wore
Hats to doff at gentry, the landed gits,
not even fit to shovel their stinking shit.
Born with a ring right around their heads,
the mark of the serf,
The arse-licking ones who would lie in a
puddle if their master comes.
Yes, sir. No, sir, three bags full – they
follow his instructions like a
Village fool.

'I will shag your daughter before she is wed,'
the lord and master often said,
so with cap in hand and a bow of the head
he would let the master
Take his daughter to bed.

So all the people of Bedfordshire,
the local yokels, the veg-picking
Ones, insisted that their kids should
wear a cap so the mark on

Their forehead, the Bedford ring, the symbol of
serfdom to their master's perverted whims.
'You vote Tory, you ignorant bums,'
the lord and master
Shouted at the local ones, so off with
their caps and nod of the
Head that showed off the ring as a mark of respect.

It was a fact of life in distant years that the squire of a village could have his wicked way with those girls who were about to be wed. Do you want them wicked times back? Well, get rid of this Tory sludge.

The Blood of Vincent

'Vincent! Vincent!'
Paul Gauguin screams.
'What are you doing?
You can't do that here.'
But Vincent Van Gogh
Cuts off his ear.

'You fool, you fool,
You stupid fool,'
As Gauguin sighs.
'Your sunflower painting
Is not even dried.

Paint it again.
Paint out the red.
The blood from the ear
Will turn it orange
Instead.'

Now this is the reason why
The *Sunflowers*
Are orange and not yellow.
It came from Vincent's ear –
This brilliant, demented fellow.

The Brats

Mummies' cherished little darlings
Or Daddies' handsome little chaps
But in every truth and honesty
Are nothing less than little brats,

Screaming, whingeing little toe-rags
Who grab everything they see,
Bullying other little kids with impunity.

But these mums and dads are blinkered
And point-blank refuse to see
That their little darling angels
Are the new menace to society.

Greedy selfish little tykes
With manners worse than pigs,
These little Britons of future years
So glad it's not my kid!

The Bung

With all the 'brown envelopes' full of cash (no doubt) changing hands with politicians and big business for favours or knighthoods, or just to pay off their mortgage, this poem is dedicated to the sick gits who run this nation and take us for a load of fools.

An insidious sickness now prevails
In those who govern and in power –

Some are bent like shepherds' sticks
Who take a bung with cash in it.
Corporate bodies flaunt their cash
With MPs baying, 'We must have.'
With your lolly you make the rules.
Take no notice of those voting fools.
We have big fat contracts up for sale,
Ermine peerages with all their gowns.
Make your payments in gold or cash,
Denying the fact we took your stash.
So take your pick of what you need
And woe betide the persons
Who call us THIEVES.

The Cenotaph

Where statesmen stand once a year
Heads are bowed, without a tear.
The Cenotaph is a wall of shame,
Etched with death and unknown names.

Two world wars and countless others,
Men have died for these despotic buggers.
They lie and cheat and create the wars.
Brave men died for these evil men
Who stand there in a solemn line
As war heroes slowly march on by.

They lay their wreath, a moment spent
Without a care, with scant relent.
With every name that's carved in stone
And every life that death had spent,
Their bloody hands we won't forget.

Medals shine on old comrades chests.
Now quite old and bent with age,
Now they're in their twilight stage.

They march in line and turn to the right
Just as the despotic buggers come in sight.
They raise their hands in a two-finger salute,
'Colonel Bogey' they whistle in tune,

Pointing a finger at the Cenotaph stone
And shout in unison, 'This should be your home.'

The Chemical Cosh

The old and the frail, with no voice to speak
Live in fear if hospital care they do seek.
Friends and neighbours never come home.
A pine box is waiting with handles of chrome.

For if you go into hospital or a nursing home
Your aunts and uncles, your mums and dads
Who celebrate longevity with the life they've had,
Beware my friends, if you're old and you're weak,

They will bump you off, with a nod and a wink.
The chemical cosh guarantees the long sleep.
Once they've injected you with this psychotic drug
All your crying and moaning will suddenly stop.

Goodbye, you old ones, for this is your lot.
Heartbeats will cease like an unwound clock.
So it's farewell from him and goodbye to YOU too
As the angels of death come after you.

*Antipsychotic drugs are as follows: Zyprexa, Risperdal,
Seroquel. Look out for these names on the record sheets
of your loved ones. Scream blue murder for the antidote
then sue the pants off the gits
    who tried to kill them. This was highlighted some
years ago and it still goes on!*

The Children of Greed

We don't care for kith or kin
Paying lip service with a grin.
We don't say those little things,
Simple words that mean a lot
To mums and dads, WE forgot.

LIKE...
We love you, Mum, and you, Dad.
Please forgive us, we forgot.
You're in our thoughts, night and day.
It costs us nothing, these words to say.

BUT...
We never phone or visit you,
Selfish and careless, this is true,
But we will see you when you DIE
To grab your wealth, your son and I.

AND...
You never knew, Mum or Dad,
We are not the children you once had.
We grew up in a grabbing world
Without the values you always had.

'Thatcher's Children' they call us now
Who follow the ways of that wicked old cow.
We grab and gobble all we see,
No place for love in the children of GREED.

*The moral of this tale is this: spend it all whilst you
can before the birds of prey pick over your bones.*

The Concourse of Life

All life is here as you wander around, as you
Circle and browse the shops that abound.

A fresh cup of tea or coffee from abroad a
Taste of the Orient for Amigo you might be.

Buy your newspapers or sweets from their shops,
Amigo will have it whatever you want,
From this wonderful food hall they stock a whole lot.

Sit at the tables with crowds milling round,
Patients and visitors, nurses and docs,
As they go round the concourse to various shops.

Flowers from Tolly's, a lovely bouquet of flowers
For a loved one on visitors' day or just
A haircut or a Body Shop shampoo,
Whatever you want, you have only to choose.

A quiet place to pray for a loved one in need,
Of the spirit and mercy from the god that you plead.
The chapel is there for all to partake in,
The wishes of prayers your god did create.

Even a bank and a money machine and even
A market that sells everything,
You will find it all in this circle of life,
The concourse in Addenbrooke's, this hospital of fame,
That treats one and all in our great National Health
Service name.

The Cry of the Whale

Deep in the oceans
Of all seven seas,
Dolphins and whales
Roam around free.

They know about man
With his barbaric ways,
His taste for carnage
And mammals' blood,

Who butchers and maims
With harpoon guns,
Blowing their insides
To kingdom come.

Why do you do this
To mammals of the sea?
Do they not know
They give birth to live babies
Who suckle on milk
Till their early teens?

They've roamed this planet
Over millions of years.
The species called humans
Are their greatest fear, they

Bring death and destruction
To our friends of the deep.

The seas are their home,
All seven oceans they keep.

So wherever they may roam,
Please let them be free.
Give them a chance
In the depth of the seas.

The Curse of Thorns

The crown of thorns that
Crowns his saintly head,
Thrust on tight so much
Pain and blood is shed.

Pinned to a cross by feet
And hands by rusting nails,
Skin, flesh and bone.
'Mercy,'
The crowd does cry, to no avail.

Left to die on that wooden cross
For sins of humankind, long
Forgot. 'Father,' he cries, 'they know
Not what they do.' But his father,
God almighty, curses all of you.
You murdered his child, his only
Son, and he is making you pay,
Each and every one.
A pox on your souls till the end of time,
With wars and famine and mothers
Who weep for sons who are butchered
By sick human freaks.
So it is said, so it is done.

The Dark Side of Life

As a child, and one of eight,
I knew the meaning of
A parent's hate.

For some unknown reason
I did not fit.
Odd bod, the family freak,
Pee the bed, the whipping boy,
The ugly figurehead.

Nothing but hate
In my first years on earth
From a mother
Who wished I had died at birth.

In those long tormented years
I cried a vast ocean
And a river of tears.
My screams of pain
And pleas to stop
But the beatings
On bare flesh
Was a pleasure she got.

A sadistic woman, with pure
Hate in her eyes,
Burned me with pokers,
Nearly beat me to death.

Shut me in a coal cellar
At the height of the war,

Hoping the Germans
Would blow me to bits.
Some kind-hearted neighbours
Rescued me from it.

The beatings went on
In the dark youthful days
By a woman called mother
Who called me a freak.
Depression, malnutrition,
Unloved and quite weak.

She despised her young son
For reasons unknown
But sadly I find
A black sheep
In lots of our homes.

The Darkest Years

Do you remember long ago
As a child of eight or so?
'Spanish wood'
Was all the rage
When sweets were rationed
Like utility clothes.

Speckled apples,
Stale old cakes
For one old penny,
A feast you'd make.
Tuppenny cornet,
Big round block,
Fantastic taste
I've not forgot.

Herbal tablets, 'Nippets' too
Were sweets not rationed
To war kids true.
Ration books of Es and Ds
Brought any sweets
You'd like to please.

'Bagwash shop' on a Friday night:
Collect the washing
In a two-wheeled cart
Or a ball-bearing scooter
Made of wood, along the pavement.
They'd sound good.

Powdered egg, dried-up prunes,

Jars of malt, you'd get one spoon.
Bread and dripping, a mug of tea,
Were make-do dinners for you and me.

War was raging at this time
With buzz bombs flying
Overhead. If the engines stop,
A street is dead.
Air-raid warning, banshee sounds,
Like a rabbit you're underground.

Searchlights blazing overhead,
Ack-ack gunners bombarding lead.
On with masks in case of gas
When enemy bombers begin to blast.

'Blackout curtains,' a man would shout,
If a speck of light should shine out.
The air raid's over, the street's alight.

A landmine fell within the night.
Devastation all around
All that's left is scorched
Black ground.

The darkest years I knew so well
When birds of death rained down hell.
Go down deep, deeper still
Away from bombs and shrapnel shells

Some happy memories, but most are sad,
for this is what
Happens when the world goes MAD.

Wartime Britain 1939/45.

The Darkness of Dartmoor

This ancient county with the Devonshire moors
From Westward Ho to Dartmouth Docks, the
County is haunted with myths and legends
So many forgot.

There is the highwayman of Beetor Cross,
His eye sockets are empty as he is often seen
Standing there on Dartmoor Green,
with a cloak and dagger and
Two flint guns to rob and plunder the frightened ones.

Again on Dartmoor, by Bradford Pool,
a female voice will gently
Call, softly calling for you to take a swim, then pull
you down
Into the deep dark pool, till your lungs
stop breathing in that deathtrap pool.

The sounds of battle can still be heard
over the Bridge of Cadover
In the dead of night when clash of swords
And shields drown out the screams
of those being killed.

Over the moor near Princetown and Ashburton Way,
The guardian monster of a treasure trove roams
Chaw Gully with ravens and crows,
Not a single soul has survived the fall,
As the monster of Chaw Gully eats their body, and all.

A mile or two near Exeter town and the Dawlish River
Where Childe's Tomb is found, this hunter of the
Dartmoor Plains,
Froze to death in the dead of night
in the month of August.
When hot and bright, they say you
can see his ghost at night,
Carried by monks in the August moonlight.

Many a tale Devon can tell of ghosts and legends
And a life in Hell but the moors of
Dartmoor are a mystic place
The horror of which many befell.

At Lustleigh Cleave on the edge of
the moors strange horsemen
Do ride in the dead of night, dragging dead travellers
to tin mine pits, then casting their bodies
down these disused tips.

At Lych Way phantom monks are seen
pulling the hearse full
Of the dead, miners of tin who were crushed to death.

Rowbrook, Broad Stones, by the river Dart,
just once a year
Will call you by name and take away your fears.
'Come swim in my water. It's lovely and clear,'
then drown you
And dump you on a far distant shore, lifeless meat,
a human no more.

Beware of the pixies from Cornwall way
who came to Devon in
The coffins of slaves, small and evil,
who loiter in your way,
Digging deep holes in the moor's vast grounds,
Them fill them with water so the visitor drowns.

But all in all, it's not a bad place, this Devon of mine,
This beautiful place. The stories are
true so be on your guard
For we want your money before
you reach the graveyard.

The Dawn of Armageddon

Sleepwalking nightmare
But this one is true –
No snow on the ice cap,
The melt is down to you.

Earthquakes devastate China
Bursting man-made dams,
Flooding the whole of Asia,
Typhoons drowning man.

Tidal waves from Noah's
Ark of biblical times –
Waters from the oceans
Left it on a mountainside.

Searing heat of desert sands
That swiftly turns to glass.
Molten sand of half the world
Evaporates everything in its path.

Trees have gone, long ago –
Spontaneous combustion.
See how brightly we will glow
Along with fish in boiling seas.
Not a single life form will survive.
The dawn of Armageddon
Is just about to arrive.

The Day of Reckoning

Who on earth can defend these thieves
As the day of reckoning comes to pass?
For those who stole by dirty deeds
The lifeblood of humanity's needs,

Taking the bread from children's mouths,
Removing the people from their homes,
Foreclosing, disposing as worthless, trite,
The dreams of millions all over this world.

They feather their nest with billion dollar bills
As we mere mortals must swallow this pill.
But the day of reckoning has come to be
When the nations of earth catch these thieves.

Take it back, all that they stole
Then drop the lot into a big deep hole
Where the devil himself can have their souls.

The Dentist (Dr Costalot)

This poem is dedicated to those greedy gits who pull teeth. Their greed knows no bounds, charging for the dental care of young kids and hard-up pensioners.

I put them in the same league as
Politicians, estate agents, solicitors, all of whom
Rip off the British people with impunity –
And bankers.

Tooth decay or septic gum,
Phone the dentist for here I come.
If you're lucky, you've picked the best,
Trained and paid by the NHS.

He takes a look at your rotten tooth
Sticking a spike in as you hit the roof.
'Does that hurt?' you hear him say.
Yes it does, so how much do I pay?

'Welllllll,' he says, as he rubs his hands,
'You pay a fee for different bands.
Private work will last and last
But the NHS is in another class.
We use the best, the private way.
NHS are back the next day!!!'
'Is that fair?' I complain to him.
'It should be equal on both the schemes.'
'Don't be stupid,' he winks at me.
'How do I keep my yacht at sea?'

The Destroyers of Hope

So easy to control all those who walk
Without hope, pushing aspirations onto
A violent downward slope, turning honest
People into the rich ones' passive slaves,
Guttersnipes of government are so
Busily engaged.

Fascist little Eton scumbags that hold the
Public purse who are just as bad as Hitler
Or Goebbels at his very worst, punishing all
The poor ones at the bottom of this human
Heap, shamelessly embracing austerity days
Of labour on the cheap.

The citadels of monetary corruption that now
Infect our lands, bankers grabbing our money
With both their snatching hands. MPs look on
At bankers, just watching these scum who thieve
As they line their stinking pockets with loot that's
Yours and mine, scrapping laws that protect the
Rich from prosecution of their crimes.

Hope is now fading for Britain's hard-pressed
Low-paid working class as thugs from the Halls
Of Crime and Corruption whip your fu*king arse.
The bolshie ways of the 1960s is not seen in
Thatcher's children of today.

Brainwashed by the Maggot that greed is good for you,
Just let the poor ones pay. Doff your caps of cloth
And cringe and fawn as you work until you drop,

Or fight the right-wing bastards. Never let them win.
Hold the banner way up high until we oust this
Fascist lot.

The Devil Rides Out

If you gaze into his eyes
The horrors of this world
Are etched inside.

Unholy deeds they have seen,
Butchery and death, needless greed,

The killing fields of Cambodian plains,
The genocide of millions
In unmarked graves,

Ethnic cleansing, tribal hate,
Religious bigots of every faith,
These despotic humans he creates.

The devil rides out to cast his net
Over the monsters and tyrants
Not named yet.

The Devil's Seed

Just look around you,
Tony Blair.
Turn your head;
See what you've done,

Just you and Bush,
Satan's other son.
Are you deaf,
Blind and dumb?
Can't you see
The carnage going on?

You don't care
Or give a blind fig that
Brave men died
For the things you both did.

You spun a yarn
So very very long,
Fooled the world
With your disaster songs

But all along
You made us all think
Iraq could bomb us
And make us extinct.

Black Gold, Texas tea,
The killer oil

You were after
In Iraq's sovereign soil.

A bloody war
Is what you pair got.
Thousands will die
In the name of greed
As Bush and Blair
Scatter their fathers' seed.

The Drummer Boy

Into the battle with his rat-a-tat-tat,
Leading his legions with rat-a-tat-tat,
No weapons he carries, rat-a-tat-tat,
On the fields of carnage, rat-a-tat-tat,
Beating his battered drum, rat-a-tat-tat,

Rat-a-tat-tat.

Army drummer boys beat out the pace
As brave young men engage the foe.
A drum for a weapon as into battle he goes,
Tapping the beat to the soldiers' marching feet.
Cries of valour as onwards they go and no retreat,

Rat-a-tat-tat.

A cowardly dark enemy took the drummer boy's life.
They butchered the young man with hatchet and knife.
'Allahu Akbar,' they screamed,
as they finished the foul deed.
It shamed all Muslims who follow
the Koran's creed,

Rat-a-tat-tat.

Bow your heads in shame if you
speak this drummer's name.
He died dressed in civies on our
streets one dismal May day

349

By the hands of Muslim maniacs
who took his life away.

RAT-A-TAT-TAT.

For Lee Rigby.

The Enemy Within

Within our shores we have British-born foes
Killing our nation with political hammer blows.
They are hammering the poor and the
Underclass, saving their personal wealth and
The banking class.

Wholesale moral corruption of the established
Elite, the monarchy and Parliament to lords who
Cheat but in truth it's them should pay for the
Deeds of banks whose trillions are hid away, making
Sure they never sink.

But the poor, the old, the sick and the weak pay
A big price for these vile and uncaring, disgusting
Establishment freaks who couldn't care less as
You pay the bill for banking cheats, for the vile
Enemy within is those who rule – from the monarchy
And Parliament to Parliamentary fools.

The English Haggis

So the wee toady Scotsman has told us porky
pies for the English cooked the first
Haggis in 1615 long before a toady Scotsman
had ever seen one.

It came from England, the English *husewif*,
the recipe for haggis, this gut full of stew;
It never was Scottish for it didn't belong to you.

Some hundred years later in 1747
some Scotsman tasted
Our Haggis and said it was heaven,
so he ran back to Scotland with a
Haggis under his hat, laid it on a kitchen
table and told his clan he had cooked that.

They did a jig and a Highland reel to celebrate
this find but he
Never let the truth be said: it was
England's all the time.

The Fable

Your Country Needs You. Sorry folks, but here is another protest poem.

Wars are fought for the privileged few
Who goad you on 'behind the queue'.

These sick little men, with twisted minds,
Who sing out the songs of barbed wire and mines.

'Give your life in blood and sweat.
Your life today we will not forget.

Your country needs you, young or old,'
This fable sung by men of old.

But heed these words, do not bother
You're nothing more than cannon fodder.

They promise the earth if you win the war
But you end up crippled, disabled and poor.

THEY want the wealth of others' lands
Like gold or oil in desert sands.

So question that fable your fathers sung.
YOU don't have to use the bayonet and gun.

If THEY want a war, give them your gun
Put THEM in uniform and watch them all run.

The Family Silver

'Twas long ago, just after the war,
A UK government that pledged and swore
We would no longer pay for health,
All dental care would be free
And a state pension for you and me.

But many a billion this would take
To fund the money for a welfare state
So the wisest men of that day
Looked around for who should pay.

So the richest companies were made to pay
Gas and electric and water too
But these didn't belong to me or you.
All the railways, with all their stock,
Every coal mine and every pit,
The GPO, including telephones,
Would pay for it.

Now all this wealth was in private hands
Owned by the few throughout these lands
So the Labour Party of the day
Took all their wealth away.

It took from the rich and gave to the poor
The 'family silver' we adored.
Then came Thatcher, a satanic witch
Who sold it back to the ultra rich.

So if your pension is looking thin
And you smile with a toothless grin,

You have to work till you drop.
Just blame Thatcher for your miserable lot.

The Final Message

Help, the Beeb have beaten me.
They've taken my pen and scribble pad,
Bound my mouth with the censor's gag,
Taken my freedom to speak my mind,
Cast us back to those Orwell days.
Darkness descends, the world is black,
Auntie Beeb has made sure of that
Just can't believe this is true.
Did not this corporation
Belong to me and you?

Dumbfounded.

The Forgotten

Come, said Pachamama,
The mother goddess of earth,
You are the children of the gods.
Let us talk of the heaven-bound way.
This earth is not your home to stay.

You are the Inca, the star-bound ones.
Gather your children, hold them tight,
As Pachamama sings with all her might.

Listen deeply, my chosen ones,
You start the long journey to that other sun
Deep in eternity, till the end of time,
Pachamama sings of the lost Inca tribes.

The Four Horsemen

I dreamed a dream.
I spied four horses riding so very high,
Thundering across an inferno of a sky.
Cloaked dark figures on their backs,
Four great horses that left no tracks.

'Twas the great white horse of burning hate
That left the exit of Hades' inferno gates.
A conquering rider his blazing bow in hand,
That enslaved all humans, has his arrows land.

Breathing fire from the devil's red-hot pit,
A massive red horse came thundering from it,
Its bony rider swathed in fire blazing red,
A golden sword in his hand sparking off hatred
In the souls of man.

Then a black-cloaked devil who rode his steed
Straight at mankind for selfish unbridled greed.
If you see this horse of midnight black, beware you all,
You can't turn back.

A pale grey horse with blood-red eyes was the
worst of four that rode out from Satan's darkest doors.
Plague and famine that rider brought
as he rode swiftly
On all four winds.

Then I heard this call – 'Close your eyes,
cover your ears
When the four horsemen of the apocalypse draw near.
See them, hear them. It's your fate chained forever
To the devil's own gate.'

The Ghetto

Ten square miles, a squalid block
Of Victorian buildings and obsolete shops,
Blacks and yellow, red and whites,
Crammed together in ghetto blight.

Hungry kids in shabby old clothes
Pick up garbage from gutters where
Down and outs roam the streets
Or lie wrapped in newspaper on park bench seats.

Vice and violence go hand in hand
In every street of this ghetto land.
Walk the streets late at night where
Whores and pimps line the streets
Selling their bodies so they can eat.

Down the road a block away,
A drunken wino stumbles and sways,
Drinking meths from a battered can,
Nearly dead from this deadly drink,
Shutting from his mind the ghetto stink.

For once you're trapped in this hole,
Trapped forever in the legion of lost souls
Sick in body and in mind,
The very bottom of humankind,
Open your eyes and you will see
This ghetto plague around you or me.

London, 2002.

The Ghost of Christmas Bush

Once upon a time in
The land of the great dollar bill
Lived a wicked Scrooge-like being
Who spoke and caused great ill.

We must have a war, use any tricks,
Rope in Blair, the British gullible twit.
Tell him history is waiting for him.
He will be always remembered for it.

So like two fools from a Dickens tale
They conjured up this stupid war
In far-off lands and desert sands
To settle a trumped-up score.

They poured in billions
And made some ultra rich
But hundreds of brave men
Fucking died for it.

The Golden Urine Pot

They've taken the 'P'
From all of us lot,
Bankers and traders
As they count the loot
In their golden urine pot.

They don't give a damn
As the 'P' in their pot
Flows onto their hands
To buy up oil wells
In distant Arab lands.

So taking the 'P'
Out of you and me
Is like shelling peas
Instead of pea pods.
It's trillion dollar wads
Belonging to you and me.

So let's all 'P' in their pots
As we throw them inside.
Stack them in tight
Pour in OUR 'P'
Right up to their mouth
Of bankers and traders
Who stole from me.

Say 'cheese' you thieves
Go drown in drown in our 'P'

That will teach you bums
Now taste of our 'P'.

As the world urinates
To drown this scum
So drown in the waste
That comes from our tums
Bankers and traders
The non-human ones.

The Goose-Stepping Starts Again

The jackbooted thugs
Are on the march
From a period of history
We thought was dead.
The Horst Wessel
SA song is being sung
As goose-stepping thugs
March in Europe again.

The splintered sounds
Of shattered glass
As the spectre of Kristallnacht
Comes back from the past.

Another Joseph Goebbels
With twisted wicked mind
Will stir up the masses
Not for just Jews, this time.

Their hate is vented
From Europe's vast lands
To immigrants and cultures
From Middle East desert sands.

Austria and Belgium
Have joined this league
With Bulgaria and France
In this far-right team.

An ultra right-wing's
Filthy monstrous plot
To create another Adolf Hitler
With his murderous lot.

The Granny Bashers

They did their bit some sixty or so years ago,
Grandma and Granddad, as unsung heroes.
Many fought on all kinds of forbidden foreign
Shores, deserts and jungle – these brave ones
Fought our wars,

Coming back home, when the deeds were done
To a country that was unfit for Britain's fighting chums.
But socialists were swept into power, taking all the
Wealth from the upper-class shower and created
The welfare state, old labour empowered.

Grandma and Grandpa gave you the first NHS,
Plus a free dentist and a state pension, no less.
No more servitude, were our grandparents' words
As they threw off the chains of the pre-war serfs,
Giving their offspring the manners and respect
That is sadly lacking in everything we see
In today's young people's very sick society.

Now a greedy coalition government rules
granny and me
Which robs and steals our paltry
pensions with impunity.
A fascist as a leader from the school of Eton thugs
Plus a chancellor who is as evil,
making the poor ones pay,
Stealing billions from our NHS and pensions'
rainy days.

These are worse than Thatcher
and her stinking Tory crew.
Even now you can see some them robbing me and you –
Geriatric sick shits, Clarke and Ian
Duncan 'KILLER' Smith
Planning how to rob and plunder old
Granny's little pot
Which should make the whole
British nation rise up and

Tar and feather this scandalous, evil lot.

The Gravy Train

Here we go down the track,
Chuffing and puffing,

We must have,
We must have.

Stop at the station
Where vast fortunes
Are found.
Stop in the siding
That MPs gather round.
Chuffing and puffing,

We must have,
We must have.

Extra money
For a second house,
Trips to China
Or a computer mouse.
Chuffing and puffing,

We must have,
We must have.

Top-class restaurants
To gobble their food,
Hotel bills

Paid by the state,
Buckets of money,
Loads of cash.
Chuffing and puffing,

We must have,
We must have.

The gravy train
Is on the track
With MPs fighting
For your cash.
Tax-free freebie,
An MP's perks.
They've taken us all
For a bunch of jerks.

The Great British Dumpling

We are the dumplings,

Europe's stuffed pigs.

Dumpy dollops of flabby fat,

Chubby chops who don't give a fig.

Lardheads they call us, Europe's fat pigs,

Fatty dumplings not fit for stew.

Hoping my good friends this don't include

YOU.
(Seen more fat on a chip.)

The Great Depression

The gaunt face
And hopeless looks
As the Great Depression
Dug in its spiteful hooks.

Jobless millions
Of mournful souls,
Barefooted children
With rags on their backs,
Walking in circles to find
Some food as soup kitchens
Hand out gruel from a steaming pot.
One meal a day was the most
They got.

Greed of the '30s, a gold rush for some,
Brought down the nations from all over
This earth, as pigs on Wall Street made a fast
Buck, but didn't give a shit or a banker's wank as the
Rest of the world slowly sank.

Money was worthless, a big pile of junk, as
Inflation ripped away at the soul and food to eat
Was the people's main goal. Millions perished in
Those distant days but the similar familiarity is
Here today.

Greed and corruption is the ruler again, a second
depression is
Well on its way.

This poet lived through the last years the first one.

The Greedy Gene

These are dangerous times, both in
Britain and the USA and
Maybe in the whole of the Western
World for we are witnessing
An unprecedented time of greed and
corruption. The divide
Between rich and poor has
never been so great.

It seems the poor and underclass
are going to pay for the
Sickness that is Wall Street and the
City of London, both of
Which harbour the detritus of all
human life. This greed has
Infected great swathes of America
and especially the
Republican South and, with the help
of the Murdoch publishing
Empire, both sides of the Atlantic.

The low-life cretins who control
banks in our big cities have
Been diagnosed with a new gene
that was found in the genome bank
A couple of years ago and scientists
have named it, rightly so,
The 'greedy gene' which is very
apt for these low lifes.

This gene must be eradicated from
the human race for it
Blinds those who have it to all that
is good in humans for
Most would sell their own grandmother
if they could make a
Nickel or a penny for her dead body.

In Britain we have a group of bad
genes called the Eton
Mafia who are inbred throwbacks
of the lord and master days
Of Edwardian Britain. None have done
an honest day's work in
Their fetid life and hold the working class in deep
Distaste but these multimillionaires
of the Conservative
Party have formed a coalition with
a equally distasteful bunch
Of low lifes called the Lib-Dems,
who have been out of power

Since the days of the hated Lloyd
George who was the biggest
Political gangster of his time nearly
one hundred years ago.

The blame and cost is going to fall
onto the poor and underclass of
Britain. They will pay with their
jobs in the millions
And the very social fabric that
bound our country together is

Being ripped up into shreds.
Children will suffer and the old
And infirm will also pay for the
greed of the City of London
And The Wall Street banks
and stock exchange.

But we in Britain can hear the
murmurs of rebellion and civil
Disobedience against those who
push its people onto the
Breadline and soup kitchens of
despair of the 1930s and that
Murmur will turn into screams of
blind hatred against the
Pigs who call themselves the British government.

Yet those who caused this disaster
are still awarding
Themselves massive bonuses
and sit back in their plush leather chairs
And take the piss out of those
who are bailing them out.

But here is a sanguine bit of
tax-free advice for these
People infected with the 'greedy gene':
Build your walls high
Around all that you have stolen
for the whole nation will be
After your skins in a few weeks' time.
Mark this well, push the

British people's backs against the
wall and they will stampede
Over your rotten carcases just as
they did against that other
Tyrant, Adolf Hitler.

The Green 'Gilby'

This slimy green blob
Of mucus grunge
Sliding down the nose
Like a slivering snake

Which shoots up again
When a sniff you make.
But gravity rules
This innocuous blob

Which slides over the lips
And into the gob
For as a child
You must have seen
Children at desks
All covered in green.

Too late for hankies
When a 'Gilby' attacks
As it drips from the nose
And onto their laps.

The best place for wiping
This sticky green mess
Is the cuff of a jacket
Or the hem of a dress.

So when you meet
The kids from school

Keep your distance
From that crusty green kid

That little green gilblyGilby
May not be his!!

The Human Condition

Since the times of old
When Eve stole that apple,
A forbidden fruit from
The oldest tree in eternity.
Its fruit was the very essence,
The beginning of human greed.

Greed in all its shapes and forms
Is predominantly a human trait.
This sprang from greedy religions
Over two thousand years old,
Mind control of gullible ones
That enslaves their minds
In chains of fear and steel
So priestly unscrupulous crooks
Can take a steal.

Majestic buildings decked with gold
Collected from the brainwashed
In silver or gold or copper and brass
They take it all and laugh and laugh.

Greed is seen in history past
In wars and conflicts over this world
But religion plays a smaller part
As bandits and banks and big city crooks
Colluding with governments, the lowest of scum,
Robbing and stealing, by plunder and theft,
Billions in gold from this earth's poorest ones.

No other beast that walks earth's space steals

From their own and holds them in contempt.
To enslave a fellow human with the pound
Or the buck, or the rising yen, that can enslave
The millions with so little of them.
Your slaves of the rich, the harbingers of hate,
Who look upon the poor, the wretched underclass,
As servants and mules for the rich to kick, as the
Workers who are born to shift their shit.

The Hungry Ones

We were urchins during the war,
Dirty, filthy, unwashed kids
Living in London during the Blitz,
Scabby skin and flea-ridden hair,
A mum or dad who just didn't care.

Hungry mites in war-torn days
Who lived by their wits
To keep starvation at bay,
Thieving food from local shops,
One for all we shared the lot.

Freshly bombed-out local homes,
Urchin kids would love to roam,
Searching for things to steal,
To sell and buy a proper meal.
Some died within these crater traps
As floors gave in and roofs collapsed.

The smell of fresh roasted flesh,
Fires smouldering – the sign of death.
Urchins dig and pull and tug
A rabbit-like body roasted we did love.
The flesh is hot and tastes quite sweet
But unknown to us, it's a cat we eat.

We collect newspaper by the ton,
Brass and copper, lead and steel,
Sell it all to buy our meals.

Bread and dripping, a mug of tea
The daily diet in wartime days.

Urchins of London ate in other ways.
Steal a rabbit or milk from a cart,
Run amuck in a baker's and steal some tarts.
Raid allotments for carrots and peas,
Sell it all for the food we need –
Mostly cakes and chocolate buns
For they called us the urchins
The hungry ones.

The Impostors

This is a reality poem that affects us all, one way or another (depending on what fence you're sitting on).

You sold us all down the drain
After years of fighting in Labour's name.

We marched with banners flying high –
It was them or us, do or die,

But along the way you lost the plot.
You've dumped us all, the working lot.

You sold our 'silver' to the highest bid.
You've sold it all to wealthy PIGS.

You make us sick, with your Tory ways –
Council tax, petrol tax, to name but two,
A burden created by your stinking crew.

Many a pensioner goes cap in hand
Along the length of this rich man's land.
You're not the Labour of the working class,
You suck the detritus from the rich man's arse.

They are the ones who pull the strings
That makes your mouths jerk and sing.

We've had enough of your Blairite ways.
Your time has come to leave your seats

And get out of our sight, you TORY CHEATS.

The Index Finger

This little poem came to mind as I was waiting in a queue and watching the bloke in front of me
Picking his nose, then tapping his pin number into that altar to the money gods, the pin machine,
One of the filthiest things we use. Read on.

Beware ye all, the index one
This digit that's used by everyone.
Did the person in front
Wash his hands
With soap and water
Before tapping his pin
On the pin machine altar?

His nose-pickings will stick
To your fingers and thumbs
If his pin numbers
Are similar to your ones.

So wash your hands
When leaving that shop
Or catch something nasty
That person has got.

Just imagine in your mind
Where his fingers have been
Before he used
That pin-number machine!

The J Arthur Bankers

J Arthur Banker,
You sick
Disgusting gits,
Where did you find
Your British morality?
In a pigsty dung heap,
Steaming horseshit pit?

You all should be in prison,
The whole thieving lot ,
For billions went on
'WALKIES'.
This stash that
Was never found –
We should dig up
Your ruddy gardens
Where you buried it
In the ground.

NOW you want a bonus
For fucking up us lot.
Let the nation kick your arse
You J Arthur Bankers
Dogshit lot.

The Jaw Bone

The mandible bone
In the female head

Can torture the male
Until he is dead.

With jawbones built
For maximum speed

To nag and jabber
For her every need.

Glowing red in full flight,
Her jawbones rattle
Till the dead of night.

Talking, squawking,
All day long,
Rabbit and rabbit
A monotonous song.

Put on your headphones
To blast out the din.
Give her some Sellotape
To tape up her chin.

PS: This is just a giggle, girls. I don't mean it. (Really, where can I get some Sellotape?)

The Labour Swan Song

Just one more chance to prove we are not really Tories,
To show you that we do care for you, please.

Just one more chance.

Just one more chance to do all the things we didn't do,
To put right the harm we caused all of you, please.

Just one more chance.

Just one more chance to show you we are repentant,
To pay back all we stole from you, please.

Just one more chance.

Just one more chance to give the pensioners their
justified dues,
To return the money we stole from you, please.

Just one more chance.

Just one more chance to spell out the real socialist
dream,
To abandon the myth of the Conservative cream
and stop the
Privatisation of everything, please.

Just one more chance.

We know the meaning of repentance,
the hairshirts we are
Wearing tell you so. We don't want to lose
our cushy number
But only the voters can make this so, please,

Just one more chance

To vote us back one sunny day to reinstate our
disgusting pay.
Please, just one more chance.

*With thanks to Bing Crosby who gave me the idea for
this from his 1930s song* 'Just one more chance'.

The Land of the Damned

The curse of greed has blighted our shores.
The English nation is not recognisable anymore.
Diluted genes and strange-looking faces
Have invaded our land from far-off places.

They've blighted our culture with fabulous wealth,
A wealth that corrupts and turns humans into thieves,
Allowing these strangers in to England to
do as they please.

Stealing our homeland, our homes,
offices and our shops
Erecting great mosques and synagogues for the Jews
That is diluting the fabric that made our country great
Disregarding the many for the wealth of the few.

London has been sold to oil-rich
Russian and Arab states,
Evicting the indigenous from
council-run Westminster flats
As filthy rich millionaires from China,
India and Bengal
Buy these dwellings to leave all the
tenants nothing at all.

'Move on,' these foreigners shout
at the old English ones left.
'Take all your belongings and
garbage and move it away,'

These foreigners shout, 'because
you've no home to stay.'

The land of the damned is not England no more
As hoards of foreigners invade England's shores.
Tell your politicians England is not for sale.
If they don't understand this message
Then throw all them in jail.

The Little Red Book

Mao Zedong would turn in his grave
If he witnessed the turmoil
The new leaders have made.
They've ripped up his red book,
A bible to some
And given all the wealth
To the elitist ones.

This communist state
That Mao did create
With equality for all
As the golden rule –
But power has corrupted
The greedy old fools.

Labour is cheap
With a billion and one,
The poorest of people,
The cheapest bar none.

Globalisation, this sickest of names,
Which has turned the Chinese people
Into western CHEAP SLAVES –
So look in Mao's red book
My downtrodden friends.
Kick out the fat cats
Who cream from the top.
Start a new revolution,
Get rid of this lot.

The Lonely Old Man

Not a soul ever knew
The burdens he bore,
His life and existence
All heartache he saw.
He carries it with him
Wherever he goes,
Even to death's door.

Like so many we see
That pass by and by,
Nondescript old humans
Who shuffle along,
Not a glance is given;
They just didn't belong.
He had a family
Who cast him adrift.
His usefulness is over
Like many of the old,
Now total misfits
In your midst.

The lonely old man
Has a story to tell
Of a life spent on caring
For the ones that he loved,

Of misguided trust for
The family of 'takers'.

Not one of them gives
The love and affection

This old man often did.

So as you go upon your way
Pass a fleeting glance
Down your life's highway.

The Lonely Shepherd

On windswept hills
The lonely shepherd
Tends his wandering
Flock of hillside sheep,

Just him and his dog,
His four-legged friend,
Fleet-footed at his hand.
Just a call or whistle,
His dog will understand.

His days are long
Upon these hills
But he plays Pan's pipes
To soothe his flock,
Tunes of old, not forgot.

The haunting sounds
Echo the hills and dales from
The lonely shepherd.
These sweet and tender
Sad and lonely sounds

Come forth from the hillside
Where he plays
the pipes of Pan
Of yesterday.

The Lord's Prayer (In Cockney Slang)

Our pot & pan, Lawd above who is in 'eaven,
Lawd above! hallowed be your handle.
All right, geezer, yaaah kingdom come.
Lor'luv a duck, you'll be done, good and proper
On my turf, as it is in 'eaven.
Gis us our daily bread and dripping.
Forgive us our barney-rubble and sins
As we turn a blind-eye to the other geezers'.
Lead this geezer from temptashun
And keep us from Old Nick
For your gaff is power and glory
Forever an' ever. Amen, nuff said, yeah.

The Manure Syndrome

Keep 'em covered
Up to their necks.
Add plenty of farmyard
Stinking dung.
Bury them deep
Every last one.

Keep 'em in the dark
At what you do.
Don't let the serfs grasp
A single clue.

Add more shit and trample
It down as we steal and cheat
All that they own.
Water the shit
So the serfs just drown.

The manure syndrome
Is this government's
Tool to rob and steal
And cheat all of you.

Your pensions they rob
As they cover you in shit
And put up your retirement
Age so you can have
Just have a sniff of it.

They dip you in dung
That covers your heads

When preaching the lies
That the NHS is dead.

Arseholes from the Lords
Who belch from their arse,
'American health is good for you',
As they take fat bribes
And with a nod and a wink
They sell off our NHS
To Yanks who cover you with shit.

They shovel in the dung
And any old shit to ethnic-
Cleanse the posh gits' pads
By hiking up the rents of
London's poor
Who are forced to move
To crapheap homes of manure
And shit

So rich stinking Arabs can grab
The homes that are left
And get you serfs to clean up the mess.

Then they set you up
One against one
As your bosses decide who
To sling in the dung –
On the dole without
Any pay and forced to eat shit
They throw your way.

As the manure syndrome
Makes you shit-eating slaves till
Your very last days.

The Memory Book

There are many things we will see
As we pass through time and our history:

All life or death, all joys and woes
As our memory bank just grows and grows.

The silver spoon or ragged sack,
We have no choice in this stark cold fact

But all our memories are blank books
From the mother's womb and the steps we took.

We fill the pages of the book of the mind
With the complex issues of humankind,

Of happy days when growing up
Or the painful memories of a beaten pup.

We write them down, one by one,
Blurring with time as it marches on.

A trillion things you might see and do,
Only stark memories will remain with you.

The strongest thoughts remain in your mind
Like how cruel and wicked is humankind.

We might mourn for mums or dads
Or shed a tear for a pet, once had,

But we are lucky in our 'cotton wool' land.

We have a chance to write our book
The memories of life so thoughtlessly took,

For as I speak and write this down
Children of the world are dying right now.

They had no chance to write their book
As they starve to death from the food we took,
Or are blown to bits by bombs and shells
In the quest for wealth from THEIR oil wells.

The Men in Grey

These pompous men whom we choose to rule
Are nought but puppets, one and all.

It's not them who pull the strings
That makes their mouths jerk and sing.
They are told what to say
By faceless men dressed in grey.

Civil servants, there are many,
Who take a cut of every penny.
They are the rulers of your life
In times of plenty and in strife.

Ten or twenty, that's the number
Who pull the strings
While governments slumber.
These faceless men we never see
Who make the rules for you and me.

It's a fact, have no doubt,
They've not a clue of what life's about.
Should there be these faceless men?
Did you vote for one of them?

For whatever party is in power,
The strings are pulled
By this faceless shower.

The Miner's Lament

Sweat and toil, lift and strain
Oh, my god, body's in pain.

Wife and kids sick in bed,
Got to work so they are fed.

(Chorus) Swing that pick, shovel that coal,
Give me strength in this cold
Black hole.

Can't give up for life's too dear.
Death's the thing that all we fear.

Take my sleep when I can.
Lift my head and it's work again.

(Chorus) Swing that pick, shovel that coal,
Give me strength in this cold
Black hole.

Work I do is hard and grim.
With the load I bear, I can't give in.

A mining man is what I am.
Dust and sweat in my blood.
Up to my neck in dust and mud.

(Chorus) Swing that pick, shovel that coal,
Give me strength in this cold
Black hole.

This breed of man with backs all bent
Who work the coalface to pay their rent.
Corns and blisters, hard work and pain
Are every miner's middle names.

(Chorus) Swing that pick, shovel that coal,
Give me strength in this cold
Black hole.

So if you're willing to do my job,
Give this prayer to your god:
'Give me strength and make me fit
To face the perils down that pit.
It's not my fault that I'm poor,
So let me see the daylight
Just once more.'

(Chorus) Swing that pick, shovel that coal,
Give me strength in this cold
Black hole.

Ministry of the Deaf

Wake up, you cretins,
Can't you hear our pleas
For armour and weapons
To fight this bloody war?

For you dumped us here
Without knowing the score,
You sick little cretins.
You've not got a clue –
Khaki suits won't stop bullets
That are fired at you.

We wear the boots
From a bygone war
That make our
Feet bloody and sore.

Our weapons are duff,
Won't work in the sand.
Our radios are crap
On old analogue wave bands.

Civil servants of carnage in
The Ministry of Death.
Arrogant cretins,
Deceitful gits,
Go drown yourselves

IN YOUR OWN TOM-TIT.

The Money Tree

The money tree is dead and gone
MPs wail in a loud moaning song.
No more freebies or cleaned-out moats,
No more caviar, just Quaker Oats.

Mortgages on ghost-like pads that are
In the pockets of these Jack the Lads.
The fruit has gone from off this tree,
You thieving MPs stole it from the

Likes of me.
White goods and the odd TV, the list is
Endless. You took from our money tree.
You put in your fingers and pulled out a plum

Then raised up two fingers to us voting ones.
So it's out on your heads and a kick up the arse.
The people have spoken, we will change it at last.
Tear up the rulebook that's three hundred years old,

Demolish old Parliament for it's time to be bold.
Bring in the new and chuck out the old,
MPs and Lords, the whole fkucing lot,
To look for their morals that most
Have forgotten.

The Morris Dance

Dancing and prancing, men in white dress
Bashing each other with bladders of sheep,

Amid great laughter at these queer antics.
Covered in flowers, all colours and hues,

Masses of bells on their hats and their shoes,
Locals and yokels who must be quite thick

Who end their dance with a fight with sticks.
The local police turn a blind eye

To bladders and sticks and men in white dress
As they batter each other, nearly to death!

(Well, we are English, what do you expect?)

The Nano and Pico Tribes

Scientists have just discovered them,
Using electron microscopes to see
Two tribes of sub-miniature humans of
Intelligence so advanced to you or me.

They've been on earth
Since time began,
Nano and Pico,
The ultra little ones.
They live within
Our very skins,
Monitoring what we do
And where we've been,
Making a logbook
Of all our sins.

Nano is the female one;
Pico is the manly one.
Together they roam
Our bodies at will,
Flitting from place to place
As every organ they embrace

In your heart or your brain
Eyes and ears, your little toes –
They even populate
Our running nose,

Migrating to other
Human ones
When mating and pregnancy

Has been done.

Their greatest fear
When you're passing wind –
Fried to death
In a hot airstream.

So remember each time
You pass some wind
Nano and Pico
Will not survive
The hot winds of hell
From your insides.

(Please stop eating hot curries.)

The New Philosophy

Kick them and starve them.
Make them your slaves.
Take all their benefits
For the rich ones to keep.
Make them bend down
To kiss their masters'
Feet.

Screw them and stuff them.
Fill them with false hopes.
Take away the safety net
So the scum just choke.
Privatise everything –
Let them freeze to death.
Do nothing to stop it,
Just pile on the crap
As they beg for mercy
We can tape up their
Traps.

For we are the New Order
That Thatcher decreed.
A nation of grovelling serfs
That panders to upper-crust
Needs.

Eton has schooled us:
'You are born to rule'
Because only us rich

Can govern these
Underclass FOOLS.

Plebs should be seen
But be silent as a grave
As they pander and grovel
To our every need,

For we are the Conservatives
Who have lied through our teeth.
We have saved all of YOUR loot
In the banks that WE own
That keeps us in great comfort
In our vast stately homes.

So raise that cap and bow your heads.
Pay homage to us as we steal your bread.
Be thankful for the jobs we grudgingly give
To you serfs and plebs we treat as pigs,

For the New Philosophy is here to stay
Because this Conservative Government
Want it that way!

The NHS

From the cradle to the grave is just a joke
When our NHS cries out, 'We are broke.'
So where have all those millions gone?
Blair and Brown, you told us lies.

Imaginary millions are pie in the sky.
Now you see it, now you don't.
We, the British, didn't enjoy this joke.

People are dying through your sleight of hand,
A pair of devious twits, detritus from a toilet pan.
You have the millions to bomb in others' lands,

Creating death and carnage in desert sands,
And you have the will to kill and plunder
But lack the will as the NHS goes under.
A fitting epitaph for this gruesome pair:
'Here lies two creatures who did not care.'

The Noble Tribes of America

The Abenaki people of New England way
For thousands of years they've been on this land,
Fishing and hunting and eating wild boar,
Gathering fruits from the forest floors.
Disaster struck two millennium ago –
The white man sailed to his shores
And the Abenaki people are no more.

The Bayougla tribe where the Red River runs,
Flocks of turkeys they bred and ate.
Red Post was their ancestral home,
Baton Rouge as it is known.

The Erie nation, a mystic race,
They roamed the land from place to place.
Their roots and origins are quite unknown
For most of the stories are home-grown.

Huron warriors of Canadian stock,
One of four of Iroquoian-tongued tribes
Who fought the British to survive,
A fearsome fighter the French once said,
Would not give in till all were dead.

The Iroquois warriors of the American plains
Who cut their hair the Mohawk way,
A fearsome tribe in many ways
Who cannibalised all they slayed.

The Nauset people from Columbus days
Living on the coastline, New England way,

A friendly tribe, they were not.
Distrusting Pilgrims and their God,
They killed and plundered quite a lot.

The Noble Red Man (Variation)

Abenaki, the first of the many, for over ten thousand years they inhabited

The New England state, gathering food from the forest floor, till the white man knocked at their door.

The Bayougoula tribe where the Red River runs, flocks of turkeys they breed and eat. Red Post was their ancestral home, Baton Rouge, it's now known.

The Chickasaw, the first of five in the Civilised Tribes, they backed the Brits to beat the French but backed the Rebs in the Civil War and the Chickasaw nation was no more.

The Delaware tribe of Moravian stock, Pennsylvania was their home. Ninety red folk were slain one night; women and kids were battered to death, Christian converts, the whole sorry lot.

Erie peoples – not a lot is known. The Dutch and Swedes did trade with them. The Jesuits and the Huron tribes tell the stories, mostly home-grown.

The Huron, now of Canadian stock, are one of four Iroquoian-speaking tribes. 'Rough and ready,' the French once said, 'A fearsome fighter. Will not give in till one is dead.'

Iroquois warriors of the American plains, who cut their hair the Mohawk way, could run from dawn to dusk and do battle on his way.

The Mohican tribe of James Fenimore Cooper fame
who penned the Mohicans' name. He was wrong to say
they were

Dead; they live and flourish in Wisconsin state, the
Stockbridge Indians they create.

The Nauset people from Columbus days who lived on
coastlines the New England way, a friendly tribe, they
were not distrusting Pilgrims and their god – killed and
plundered quite a lot.

Ottawa nation down Michigan way, remember the box
the British gave: 'Don't open it till you're at home.'
These trusting people did obey, and then died in their
hundreds from a smallpox plague.

Pocumtuc people of New England were a farming clan
– fertile land, full of game, rivers to fish and others to
meet on the Mohawk Trail.

Shawnee Nation at Fort Pitt were given blankets with
smallpox on them. This little gift they took with grateful
glee, but a nasty death came to the nation of the Shawnee.

Tsalagi-speaking Cherokee Indian was proud and aloof.
They hated the white man and his filthy ways. They
viewed not washing with utter disdain – a good-looking
race of the Indian tribes, not ugly as the whites they
bitterly despised.

Winnebago Indians were self-assured; they flaunted
their flair for beautiful things on clothing and objects

like butterfly wings. This skill is still seen till this present day.

There are more of the noble tribes and one day I will write them down in a rhyming prose.

The Odd Bods

We, the human race have no part
In nature's place.

Death and corruption is the trademark
Of this demented beast who
On human flesh does often feast.

Concrete and tarmac covers the land,
Where wonderful trees once did stand.

The oceans are polluted, all seven
Seas, and the fish are cancerous
And full of disease when mankind
Dumps his chemicals whenever he pleases.

The ice caps are melting at alarming rates
Because of the pollution these odd bods do make.
Rivers of blood and putrid flesh,
Blown to bits with cannon and gun,
The odd bods call this a war that
Will never be won.

They call on a god that has never been seen,
Just one of hundreds of the odd bod's human being.
Just a mind-control trick that keeps odd bods in check
When butchering each other with blood up to their
necks.

Nature is warning that it's had enough.
Time for odd bods to vanish in flames,
As the earth splits open from the north to the
South when nature erupts and opens its mouth.

Lava will flow and ash falls like rain,
To wipe out the odd bods,
The humans' other name.

The Old Soldier's Song

How many of you old squaddies know this song to the tune of 'Sorrento'?

Handing in my boots and gaiters,
Handing in my best BD,

I have finished with the army,
No more soldiering for me.

No more waiting at the guardroom,
No more waiting for a pass.

You can tell the sergeant major
To ram his pass up his arse.

Sign on again, old soldier.
Sign on again, get 'Daffy Ducked'.

I have finished with the army
No more soldiering for me.

The One-Eyed God

'Tis Odin the one-eyed god
Who gave his eye
So he could see
The wisdom and magic
In poetry.

And Thor,
The god of thunder in
Heaven, created
Tempest storms,
Gloves of iron
And the hammer of Thor,
Battling with the giants
In the tempest hail
Till of forked lighting
From his gloves
He did avail.

Then Loki,
The mischievous one,
Blood brother of Odin,
But a wizard of lies –
He lived in Asgard
Along with Thor –
Used his strength
To gain entrance to
Many a forbidden door.

Norse gods are many
In pre-Christian times.
Legends of the gods

And their mysterious deeds
predate the Bible,
Which so many believe.

To Valhalla, the hall of the slain,
You see the Valkyries ride,
Their armour so bright,
Carrying off slain warriors
To Valhalla's halls of might.

The Other Half

Give this thought, this night as you eat
Your roast beef or your turkey treats –
Half the world is starving now,
Not living off the fatted cow.

These starving millions
Of half of the world
Care not for the luxuries
Of diamonds or pearls.
A bowl of rice is all they want
From this great big world's cooking pot.

Newborn babies from the mother's womb
Add to the millions in the hunger queue.
No milk to feed them from the mother's breast
For she herself is a skeleton, no less.

A ripe old age is not for them
When starvation kills nine out of ten.
We stack our food in mountainous stocks
Sometimes left to stink and rot.
Can't mankind forget his greed
And GIVE this food to those in need?

The Peanut Club

This poem is dedicated to Sir Archibald McIndoe who saved the life of the girl I was going to marry one day – and to Sylvia, who was brave enough to marry me.

The searing pain of a burning back
This nightmare child, as the flames attack.

The hem of a dress, the flames did seek.
Fleeing and screaming to the cold black night,
The flames did burn, till blood-red bright.

This sorry child of six or so
Was sent to the hands of McIndoe,.

This famous surgeon of plastic skills
Who repaired the bodies of Spitfire crews.

The Guinea Pig Club is in their name,
The Peanut Club for kids burnt the same.

A three-year battle, a constant fight
To save the life of this little mite.

This dedicated surgeon put back the skin
Where only flesh and bone had been.

I praise this man, and his skills,
Who battled so long to save her life
For he gave me the woman
Who is now my wife.

To The Queen Victoria Hospital at East Grinstead.

The People's Party of England

It's got to be.
It's long overdue –
A new political party
Belonging to me and you.

Our stomachs are full.
We've had enough
Of stuffed shirts,
Liars and cheats
Whose promises
They never keep.

Keep your Labour
The rich men keep.
To pay less taxes
The system they beat.

Stuff the Tories,
The Liberals too.
They have nothing
In common
With me or you.

Gather the poor,
The underclass,
Gather the minorities
With no voice at all.
Shout out this message:

'Just one we are weak.
Millions move mountains –
In Parliament we speak.'

Redress the balance
My downtrodden ones.
Vote for the party
That's straight and true.
Vote for the ones
Who will look after you

The Poet Tree

You are the lifeblood of Mother Earth
That flows through your summer leaf
To give all creatures the air we breathe –
The shade we seek under the green canopy
So sweet, the gentle breeze that fans my brow,
For you are my mind, my very soul –
The wisdom that you so gladly bestow
To all humans, if only they could see it so.

The Ports of London

In the seedy ports
Of the London docks
A seaman sings
Of the things he's seen
From the wild seven seas.
He tells the wild dreams
Of seamen who live and die
Drunk as skunks
Under strange foreign skies.
In the seedy ports
Of the London docks
A baby was born
Down Silver Town way,
A whore for a mother,
Sea tramp as his dad.
The sea was his calling,
Just the one chance he had.
Eating the eyes and guts
And waste fish entrails,
Firkins of beer to wash it down
That this old sea dog ate and drank,
Made merry with whores
From Port of London docks.
Never washing, they gave
Him a dose of the pox.
Crying and loud cursing
For beer and entrails to eat,
The old sea dog danced a jig.
His bloated fat gut

Rumbles and rasps
As hot air and vile gases

Explode from his arse.

More whisky and beer,
The old sea dog sings.
Bring on the whores,
The givers of pox,
The harlots and pimps
Of London's old docks.

*This poem is dedicated to Jacques Brel and his song
'Amsterdam', the sheer power of his singing sends
goose pimples down my back.*

The Queen's Christmas Speech

As my family and I sit around a blazing log fire
After eating our sumptuous Christmas dinner,
Our thoughts and words were about my subjects
And the dire poverty my government has caused
To the disabled and so-called underclass.

That dear Mr Cameron tells me that we are all in it
Together and after we stop laughing at his stupid
Jokes I remind the oaf that I am the Queen and he
Is my servant in Parliament and he is getting above
His station in the pecking order, as I remind him not
To associate me with the serfs of my kingdom.

But on a more serious note, one should think one is
Lucky that you have a royal family who even thinks
About poverty and kids going to bed hungry and all
That peasant stuff and, as I told my prime minister,
If they are hungry let them eat cake. Then the stupid
Oaf has the arrogance to interrupt his monarch with
A story about some frog bitch called Marie Antoinette
Who said the same thing!

My family and I will make savings to placate you plebs
In so much as I reduce the servants'
wages in line with the
Minimum wage and make a charge
for rent when they use
The royal horse stables to sleep in.
Furthermore, I will tell

Charles to cut down on his household
budget and sack one
Or two of his personal valets who
wipe his backside and
Squeeze his toothpaste on his brush.
That sort of thing
Should be the job of Camilla, the
Duchess of Cornwall,
The lazy cow.

Your Queen is above this common
chit-chat of poverty and
Hunger for I leave this mundane
stuff for my ministers to
Sort out and I have asked the
BBC *not* to show programmes
Of rundown housing estates and
starving people queuing for
Food parcels and children with
rickets and scurvy picking up
Scrap food in gutters... 'Tis a bad image
to show the tourist who
Comes to see your monarchy in all
its regal rich splendour and
Not this nation's starving poor,
who are in the main feckless
And work-shy, so my minister
Ian Duncan Smith informs me.

There is no message of hope
I can give you but there is another
Royal mouth to feed and you
must pander to its every need, as

That alone should lift your spirits and
give praise that we have added
One more privileged soul to our
vast numbers who now grace the
The United Kingdom with our royal dynasty.

Merry Christmas...and do your best
to stop moaning about poverty
You never see us moaning about
such a meaningless trivial matter.
Get a job you lazy work-shy gits.
Mrs Windsor.

The RA Curse

The pain, oh, the hammer-blow pain
As rheumatoid arthritis attacks again.
Once nimble fingers and agile limbs
Are distant memories when RA begins.
A sudden ache or a stiffening limb

Or bones that hurt from deep within.
You see your doctor and he will say,
'Take these pills and it will go away.'
The pain persists, and getting worse,
But you've never heard of the RA curse.

The swelling joints on all your limbs,
The unknown fear of what this means.
A blood test shows a negative blip –
Rheumatoid arthritis has got a grip.
This dreadful disease, this painful curse
Starts crippling the body and getting worse.

Distorted fingers and twisted joints,
Toes that swell way out of shape,
Screaming torture each step you make.
The pain you feel is best described
As a six-inch nail being hammered inside.
Or your fingers crushed in a workman's vice.

The pressure increases and within its grip
The bones and sinews distort and split.
So don't dismiss RA out of hand.
RA affects both woman and man.
Life can play some evil tricks –
YOU may be the next one to suffer with it.

The Rape of the British Nation

A political rapist is on the prowl
Raping the nation of its NHS,
As sick Richard Branson
And his Virgin crew
Rip out its guts
For a billion
Or two.

Fascist con men from Parliament Square
Are raping the nation for all they are worth,
As the spawn of Thatcher, this despicable mare,
Shout out her orders to vile MP millionaires:
'Fuck 'em and rape 'em. I don't fucking care',
As they turn back the clock
To the distant dark past
Of Dickensian Britain
Of a poor underclass.

But a murmur is heard that ripples down this land
As the people rise up and shout out to make a stand
Against these bastard freaks from Parliament
Who treat us as sheep, herding us like cattle,
The sick and the poor, the homeless and weak,
Robbing us of money they pocket and keep.

Now is the time for us to rise up and say:
Enough is enough of your evil ways.
We will hunt you down and kick your arse
For we are proud and British working class.
We fought the wars for your upper crust,

Now we are turning on YOU
And trample YOU into the dust
Raping all the loot
You stole from the US…

The Rats of Bedfordshire

These four-legged creatures
That roam our streets,
Vermin that scuttle around our feet…

A bigger pest is the one in charge
Of Bedford's houses and backyards.
They've built a palace, an office block,
To house the elite of Mid-Beds council clots.

They've squandered millions from you and me
To house the chief executive who's well pleased
He's got his palace in the sky,
So rat-catching will surely die.

'We have no money for that task.
Catch them yourself, don't even ask.
If we do, we will make YOU pay
To catch those rats and cart away.'

But the biggest rats you will ever see
Are those who run local government
For the likes of you and me.

Public servants they should be
Carrying out our wishes relentlessly
But in truth they are a cunning lot.
They feather their nests, their money tree,
Retired at sixty, to hell with you or me.

The Rebellious Sixties

In the sixties we took 'them' on,
Bolshie rebels with flower-power songs.
We fought the system for our kids' lot
And won this war, against the odds
We boys and girls, the sixties Trots.

'They' thought we would buckle
To establishment whims
But striking and protesting, we did win.

We had our fill of Victorian ways
And made it clear things must change.
Our serfdom ended in those sixties days.

We broke the chains that bound us tight
To Queen and country
And the establishment might.

Now the seeds are sown in the kids we see
Who have grown and prospered since the rebel sixties.
So we gave you freedom to express your will

But! Prepare to fight and never stand still.
'They' are passing laws on 'this' and 'that'
And before you know it you're once more TRAPPED.

For as surely as night follows day

'THEY' will try.

The Rich and the Working Poor

There is a struggle going on in a
mining town in Canada
Which in respect affects each and every
one of us who
Are of working-class stock.

Corporate greed has raised its vile head on Wall Street
When Bloomberg cobbled together some ultra greedy
Bastard stockbrokers from the depth
of the human cesspit
Of life that allowed this famous
Canadian mining company
To be sold off to a Brazilian mining
company called Vale Inco.

Vale Inco has the unenviable record
of treating its workforce
like a lump of dogshit. It's done it in Brazil,
Indonesia, Russia
And all over the Third World where
labour is cheap and unprotected
From exploitation by greedy stockbrokers.

But Canada is NOT a Third World country;
it has fought tooth and nail
For its standard of living and all that it implies.

The workforce has said NO to their living standards
Being lowered to those of Outer Mongolia
or the wilds of Indonesia, and rightly so.
The Canadian government should hang
its head in shame for allowing the
Attempted undermining of its workers'
living standards
And make it illegal by law to do so.

If this struggle is not won by our Canadian working
Cousins, then other greedy bastards, subhuman
stockbrokers,
will start on YOU next. Pray that the workers will win
or see your own
Country become a pawn for the corrupt and stinking
rich scum of this world
Who will turn you into shit-eating slaves.

The River Man

Paul gave his all
In song and verse
To the country
Of his birth...
A caring socialist
For all his life,
He fled America
A country full of strife...
Evil times
In McCarthy days
When black and white
Went different ways...
So Paul came
England's way
To play Othello
On the English stage,
To tour the world
And sing his songs
'Old Man River' of
The Mississippi days...

He stood tall and
Never swayed,
Caring for others
In his socialist ways;
Gave away the fortunes
He made from songs
To the destitute and poor
In his work days long...

One of the greatest
Of America's sons,
A beacon of hope
For everyone...

Dedicated to Paul Robeson 1898-1976.

The Sackcloth World

They dressed them from
Head to foot,
A mummy encased
In a sackcloth world –
A world of heat,
An incarcerated hell.

Just a slit so they might see
All the men who prey on me,
Beasts of burden and savagery.

This Stone Age culture of days
Gone past whose females of the
Muslim faith wear the burka
Or the niqab and hijab
To hide the face
And the shayla and chador
to make them chaste.

Sexual jealousy of the Arab tribes
Cover their females from head to foot
So other human males may never look.
Stoned to death, butchered and raped,
Their every perversion they just take.

Love can never be for woman of Muslim
Fraternity lower than a stray old dog,
An insult to the human race that makes
Most Muslim men a total disgrace.

Show the world in your holy book
Where the prophet Muhammad

Was that cruel as
To give Muslim women
No rights at all.

The Second Decade of
the Twenty-First Century

So here it is, 2010. It's new so shall
we start over again? Shall we
Give back the money the firkin
bankers stole that put half of the
World on the unemployment dole?

Do we still condone all that the
City has done – they who have stolen
Vast fortunes from everyone,
who pay themselves not in nickels
And dimes or pound little coins,
this meaningless trash? They deal
In billions in great mountains of cash.

What do we do with the upper-crust
crooks who stole from the
People? From the tax that they
pay – the cost of a mortgage of a
Second home or to clean out a moat
so the ducks could roam
And put in their fingers and pull out
a plum from the tax paid by
Us all, the working class ones.

Will we condone these wars that can
never be won as our troops
Get slaughtered one by one?
Do we close our eyes at all? We see

The butchery and violence done
in the names of you and me.

When will they admit, as the Earth gets hot, that
mankind is guilty of making this so by
the destruction of rainforests or the
Drilling for oil or by the rape of the
planet and the vast seven seas?
For mankind is guilty by all that he thieves.

But when is religion, these vast
temples of wealth, going to
Preach that the world is now quite full
of millions of children who
Shouldn't be here at all, and give out
condoms to poor mums
And dads to stop over-population of
the children they must not have?

And when will the parasites who
rule you and me come down
From their towers, their fortresses
of steel and listen to us, the mass
Human race and face what they have
done as a FUCKING DISGRACE?

The Seven Political Sins

(1) Selflessness.

Lack of selflessness by holders of public office
Who dip their fingers into the public pie
And sing the song 'What a good boy am I'.

(2) Integrity.

Nod and Wink are the politician's best friends.
Integrity means nothing to mountains of cash.
Greedy and unscrupulous, you hear them bay,
'Take this peerage and give us the stash.'

(3) Objectivity.

Objectivity, now what does that mean
To someone as bent as a forging machine?
Brown envelopes are bulging with tax-free loot.
Winners take all, who gives a firkin hoot?

(4) Accountability.

Where is Blair now? Has anyone seen
This worst excuse for a prime minister that's ever been?
Accountability for everything he has ever done
Is down to us all, as he goes on the run.

(5) Openness.

'He who has the fattest wallet wins the day.
This is what openness means,' MPs will always say.
PFI may not be the cheapest or far from the best;
'Tis the best way for MPs to feather their rotten nest.

(6) Honesty.
Honesty means nothing, when the crap hits the fan.
Pointing fat fingers and hot gas from their bums,
The Speaker of the House accuses everyone.
Squandering public money so we don't have a clue
Whose fingers are in the pie belonging to me and you.

(7) Leadership.
Who said those stupid words? A leader
we've never had.
A leader has the biggest gob, a mouthy git to boot.
Those of recent years we should take
them out and shoot.
Never had a principle they could call their very own,
They find them in the dustbins around
MPs' second homes.

The Shopping Basket

Just imagine this:

Your guests are coming to your upmarket flat.
The dinner you plan must reflect your status
With that.

Melon boats for starters, a glass of rare wine,
Roast pheasant or grouse and vegetables of all
Kinds, fruit sorbet for afters, fruits from the tropics
And wines from the vine.

You fill your trolley, right to the top, luxuries and
Goodies, a mouth-watering lot.

You stand in the queue that's trailing far back. Your
Eyes gaze to the persons at your front and your back.

You look in one basket that's meagre and bland, just
four items of food you could carry by hand.

Scrag-end of mutton and onion for stew, OXO for
gravy,
A potato or two.

Their hair is quite grey; they stoop and they limp. Their
Clothing is shabby and threadbare with age now they
Are in their twilight stage.

Adjusting their glasses for a better view, they whisper
Your name, 'Hallo, son. Is that you?'

The Spiv

A 'spiv' is a spectre
Of a bygone age
Who made a living
By dubious ways.

Some made it rich
And reached the top
Just like Virgin,
Richard Branson's lot.

Now here is a spiv
Of the upper crust
Who rips off this nation
With planes and trains.
Not a soul in government
Would dare to complain.

Now Branson is up
To his old devious tricks.
He wants old Gordon
To give him the bonds,
The assets of a bank,
Taxpayers' money to
Whom it rightly belongs.

Beware, Mr Brown,
This man is a spiv.
This get-rich scheme
Is purely his.

The Sterling Years

Those of us born before 1971 will understand these words. If you're very young, ask your mum or dad.

There was half a 'quid' in bygone days.

The 'ten-bob' note was brown and frayed.

We had 'half-a-crowns', that's two and six.

And eight of them would make a 'quid'.

There was the 'two-bob' bit, or 'florin' coin.

Ten of them would make a 'quid'.

A twelvepence coin, a 'shilling' to spend.

Twenty silver coins was a 'quid' back then.

The 'sixpence' coin, all forty of them,

Would bulge your pockets with a 'quid' to spend.

'Threepence' coins, or 'thrupenny bits',

Not round or square but a funny old shape,

And eighty of them a 'quid' they'd make.

Or the 'thrupenny Joey', the real silver ones.

You found them in puddings at Xmas fun.

The 'penny' coin of copper design –

Two hundred and forty would make a 'quid'

A purse was needed with a button-down lid.

'Halfpenny' or a 'ha'penny' coin –

Four hundred and eighty to make a 'quid'.

Stacked on high, two foot tall,

To carry these coins you'd be a fool.

The humble 'farthing', the smallest of all,

Would take nine hundred and sixty

To make a 'quid'. Imagine your pockets,

If you did!

The Summer of Two Zero Zero Six

'Twas the summer of 2006
As the heatwave struck the Brits.
Temperatures rose as mercury popped,

Frying and boiling the whole ruddy lot.
People were melting in streets as they stood.
Everyone just vanished in a cloud of hot steam,

Just masses of old clothing, that's all what was seen.
Now Britain is empty, the people no more,
Just a pile of old clothing and a puddle on the floor.

The Sweetie Shop

For those of you who can still remember the shilling.

Do you remember those bygone days
When sixpence or a shilling you got paid?
This pocket money was paid to all
When sweetie shops made a beckoning call.

Rows and rows of tight-lid jars
In this little sweet shop, much admired.
Sparkling jars of coloured sweets –
You know the ones YOU used to eat...

Toffee or chocolate and candy twist,
Liquorice sticks or sherbert fizz,
Aniseed balls or bubblegum,
Blow and blow till the bubbles come.

Jelly babies or jelly beans,
Dolly mixtures and chocolate creams,
Sherbert powder as finger dips,
Your face and fingers plastered in it.

Toffee slabs, a thick brown lump,
With nut or raisins you could munch,
Humbugs and cherry drops,
Pear drops or jelly tots...

A quarter of this or two ounces of that.
Who gave a fig if they made you fat?
The smells and tastes I've not forgot.

This treasure trove of our sweetie shop.

The Sword of Arthur

Looming darkly over granite rocks up
on high the arch is seen,
the entrance to Tintagel Castle,
Arthur's home of this Cornish king.

A mystic man of Camelot times,
whose father, Uther Pendragon,
seduced another man's queen,
and Arthur became Cornwall's king.

But Merlin was not amused that
another man's wife was sorely abused.
He took the sword of Excalibur might
and cast it deep into a lake at night.

But Pendragon begged mercy for
what he had done and asked Merlin
to give the sword to his only son.

So on a dark winter's night long ago,
Merlin and Arthur waited by the deep lake
of lost souls. Merlin gave a mystic sign
as a hand did rise, the sword held tight,
as the blade did pass on to Arthur that fateful night.

'Use it well,' Merlin said, 'for if you don't,
Excalibur will strike you stone dead.'
It's the truth that unfolds here for the
Knights of the Round Table still whisper

his name – King Arthur the brave who
fights with his sword all those
who would conquer Cornwall's shores.

The Ten Contradictions

1. There shall be only one god and that is me! So say the hundreds of other religions that are on the gravy trains of mind control.

2. You can't make graven images of this being called God, so the whole world is in big trouble. Pull down your churches and other dens of worship for they are awash with graven images.

3. Don't take God's name in vain. So, since the days of the Crusades when knights of old did battle with the Muslims of the Eastern world, God has been doing battle with the same God. So who is the real God?

4. Remember the Sabbath day. Well, will someone tell the bastards who control the world's wealth that God said we must rest on Sunday and if we do work on that day we get double time.

5. Honour your mum and dad. Now that's a joke in anyone's language. Your kids rip their parents off until the pot is empty, then vanish until it's time to bury their parents and share their bounty.

6. Thou shalt not kill. Other than birth control, killing others has been the main instrument of population control but sometimes nature lends a hand in controlling our numbers.

7. Thou shalt not commit adultery. That's a hard one to keep. Since the development of the pill the whole world has fucked its brains out with every Tom, Dick and Harry, whether married or not.

8. Thou shalt not steal. So let's put every politician on this earth in prison for starters.

9. Don't bear false witness against your fellow human beings. So let's empty the world's jails of those who have been 'fitted up' to take the blame for something they never did.

10. Thou shalt not covet thy neighbour's house. Thou shalt not give thy neighbour's wife the 'eye' nor his grown-up kids, nor his car, or if they are filthy rich, his servants.

The Three-Balled Shylocks

For many years before and
After the war Britain was littered
With Jewish spivs preying on the
Weak and downtrodden poor.

Pawnshops abounded in all
London's towns. Shylock's Balls
Hung over their thieving shops,
A sign of poverty of the very poor
As worldly goods they pawn and
Hock.

Dingy windowless dumps that
Smell of fish and rancid fat, Shylock
Jews lived in that – just one window
With an iron grille to keep them safe
From all they steal.

Women would pawn their rings,
Bedclothes, their old man's shoes,
Pots and pans, granddad's gold front
Tooth, brass and copper in all its forms,
Paying the rent to other crooks who
Collect and threat.

Given a ticket with a given date and
The price you pay if your time/day was late.
They pay a pittance for all that they thieve,
Making vast fortunes on melted-down gold

For the Shylocks are back from
Times that were old.

If I was a rich man.

The Three Stooges

Moe, Larry, and Curly, whose real names are Moe Cameron, Curly Miliband and Larry Clegg, are collectively known as the Three Westminster Stooges.

All three of these slapstick goons made us all dance

To austerity's tune.

The ninety-nine per cent of us were squeezed until our pips were popped and empty shells are what Great Britain has got.

Scotland said we have had enough of the one percent of the upper crust pushing our faces into the muck and dust.

Stuff the United Kingdom and the Queen Bee too, we want independence from this motley crew.

Now Moe and Larry and Curly, on tow, went to Scotland to have their say on why bonnie Scotland shouldn't go.

But they hit a wall, a bag of bricks as the Scotts reminded them all of their dirty foul tricks.

You've ground us down to Dickensian times. You've made some pay bedroom tax and work for nothing with zero hours work contracts. You've flooded the country with immigrants who take our jobs and work a week for a couple of bob.

You've persecuted the old and frail, the disabled and weak, and hundreds have committed suicide when you stopped the payments they seek. Our children have rickets and other nasty things and go to bed hungry in Cameron's kingdom.

Our families use food banks to make ends meet and are plagued by Jewish money lenders who should be shot on sight for the interest is criminal and a shyster's delight.

So stuff you, Three Stooges, you merchants of greed, for Scotland must say yes and set itself free.

The Time Lord

He gave us time upon this earth
To set things right in nature's eyes and
Live in peace with all mankind.
Respect this earth so all may live
But the Time Lord has seen enough,

As planet by planet he turns to dust.
'You wretched creatures. You imbeciles.
Barbarous fools,' he shouts in rage.

Ripping out the chapter of the human age,
All traces of humans have gone from his book,
As the plants and the ants, the fish in the seas,
Prosper and flourish where once humans
were seen.

'The day will come,' the Time Lord said,
'I will raise two humans from the dead.
Just one more chance to make amends,
Sculptured as humans should have been.

'No eyes to see the greed and wealth,
No ears to hear religion's sorry tales,
No voice to mock those who fail and
A heightened sense of touch and smell.

'But eyes and ears and a mouth to speak,
I will give to humans if this promise he keeps.

See no evil and speak none at all.
Hear words of wisdom and cherish the meek.

'As the Time Lord, my promise I keep.'

Beam me up, Scotty !

The Village of Green

Hi folks, thinking of moving to the sticks? Well, read
This first and be prepared for the friendly welcome!

Idyllic homes in pastures green,
A dream retreat, a tranquil scene
Away from it all, or so it all seems!

Meet your neighbours, the local ones.
Been in that village since time began,
Inbred and mated over hundreds of
Years, each related in the far distant past –
Breeding that's created a distasteful typecast.

A small-minded people, who rabbit and chat,
Befriend you one minute, and then stab your back.
They hate your intrusion into their small little world
Where the talk is of pigs and cows in a herd.
YOU come from Mars or the big city scene.
Your presence is unwelcomed

In the village of Green.

The Way of Life (The Atheist Prayer)

I shall pass this way but once.
Any good thing therefore that
I can do

Or any kindness that I can show,
Let me do it now.

Let me not defer it or neglect it
For I will not pass this way again.

Sylvia Wicks (The wife).

The Windows to Your Soul

Your eyes are the windows of your soul.
You cannot hide the truth I seek
As eye to eye we both do speak.

As I gaze and travel to your mind,
I see the truth that's locked inside.

So if you're hiding some untruths,
Cast your eyes away from me
For I can see the real reality.

The Winter of 1947

Could this happen again? I was ten years old so I remember it well. Get out your long johns, lads, and start knitting those woollen knickers, girls. The big freeze is on its way again!

'Twas in the winter of '47 when the
Frost and snow did bite,

With temperatures below zero
For most of winter's nights.

The nation came to a standstill,
Encased in ice and snow,

When chilblains erupted on millions
Of hands, feet and toes.

Coal froze in the bathtubs,
All transport was standing still,

No trains came to the station
To deliver the winter fuel.

Snowdrifts as high as lamp posts
Across this ice-bound land,

The people burnt their furniture
To warm their kiddies' hands.

Power cuts were frequent
Just two years after the war.

Austerity was raging –
This hit the old and poor.

The old ones died in thousands
Throughout this frozen land,

No food was in the larder,
No fire to warm their hands.

They cried and died a lonely way,
Their bodies blue with cold.

Jack Frost held out his ice-bound hand
To kill the weak and old.

Their will to live just faded.
Their breath was chilled
No more.

'Twas the year of '47,
A year to remember well.

Nature has its funny ways
To repeat this winter's hell.

The Witches of Old England

'Twas the face of the evil witch and the howl
Of the one-eyed cat with the ghostly apparition
Of Spring-heeled Jack.

Witch-hunters of bygone days down London way
Hunted a being called ghostly Spring-heeled Jack.
Jumping rivers and row upon row of giant haystacks
As frantic Jack searched for his one-eyed black cat.

But Spring-heeled Jack is just one of the many evil ones
Treading the sod in England's lands
of King James the First
Who invoked the Witchcraft Act
of 1603 and the horror that came
To be.

In the realms of East Anglia there
spawned Matthew Hopkins,
The King's Witchfinder General,
the butcher of Satan's maidens.

From Manningtree in Essex this man
did roam, hunting witches
For the gallows tree and extracting
confessions inhumanly,
Placing the feet of the unfortunate
witch into oversized boots
As molten lead was poured into
them – Spanish Boot it was known
Back then.

Or the ducking stool that can still
be seen in many villages and towns.
By a pond or lake a stool once
stood – witches by the hundreds drowned.

Thumbscrews and the Iron Maiden,
with the horrible stretching rack,
Hopkins and others extracted witches'
confessions with all of that –

The swimming trial in which a witch
either floated or drowned,
Trussed up and flung into a pool and
if they drowned that ended it all,

But if they floated and came to the
top they were guilty of
Witchcraft and sentenced to death,
tied to two horses that ripped them in half.

They say that Spring-heeled Jack
was the lover of one and
Seen In East Anglia searching all the
known covens that used
To be, jumping and screaming frantically.

The World Just Disintegrates

As the world just disintegrates,
Outraged poets gasp in wonder.
Why on earth do other poets slumber?

Passing swiftly through cyberspace,
As one reads the crap in another place,
The world is crashing around their ears.
This talk of love and birds and bees –
Blind as bats, they refuse to see
Recession, repression at their door.
Just closing their eyes, they ignore.

They talk of ants and queenly bees.
'That bad old world can't hurt me.'
Wake up, you fools, and begin to shout.
Write your verse and shout it out.
Your soapbox has gone to ruddy pot,
Creeping poets is all you've got.
Cast the yoke from your ears and eyes
Or listen and see your artificial
World fade and die.

The World of Fantasy Art

O spirit of my
Fantasy dream,
Take me to
This wondrous
Place.
Let me rest within
Your mystic embrace.
Crush me until
We come as one.
Just let this dream
World carry on.

They Taught Them Well at Eton

Rip down Eton, the school for the toffs.
Burn down the lot, bulldoze the colleges,
The universities of hate who left their
Compassion for others at the old
School gates.

Imprison the tutors who have fucked up
Their minds, turning their upper-crust pupils,
The dross from the top, into subhuman kinds.

Memories from the past are taught by this crew,
From the days of Adolf Hitler, Himmler and
Joseph Goebbels, the peddler of hatred of Jews
And gypsies and the non-Aryan race.
They have preached this to Cameron and
Osborne who govern as neo-fascist
In Parliament's halls of hate.

Just like Adolf Hitler who hoodwinked the German
Race, driving out the poor, the workless and the old,
Cameron has hoodwinked Britain with all
The lies he has told –

Cheating kids of schooling and making them
Pay the price, cheating the disabled, the old
Ones and the poor, practising ethnic cleansing
Like Hitler did before, cutting rent allowance
That paid the filthy rich and making millions
Homeless, this shameless bastard ditched.

They taught them well at Eton to kick the
Working class, just like Adolf Hitler did to
The poor and the underclass.
Another German Kristallnacht, a night of broken
Glass, but this bunch has broken human hearts,
Trampled them underfoot and left them on the
Wayside, as a fascist we knew he would.

The traitors should be tried for treason like the ones
Who taught them thus. Burn them in a furnace and
Grind their bones to dust before he destroys our
NHS, this bastard of a prime minister
That no one fucking trusts.

Thirdborn

Beaten into a soggy mess,
Fists splash my piss-soaked vest.
The daily ritual has just begun
As the brute of a mother
Beats her thirdborn son.

Bloody hand marks, weals on skin,
Marking the body where
Callous hands have been.
Bleeding nose and swollen lips,
This evil mum knows all the tricks.

Stay away from school this day.
If they see this bloody mess
The police would knock and
This evil woman they'd arrest.

But looking back on childhood days
It's a miracle I got to this far-off way.
I know why I was beaten black and blue
By a mother who loathed and detested me.
Her firstborn, one and number two,
Were not endowed with my looks.

The sun shone from both their bums
But she wished they had the looks
Of her thirdborn son.

After all of my life has passed away,
This was the reason she hated me
So much. How sick can you get?

This Bulldog Breed

It's taken me some time since 7/7 to cool my anger at the murder in my home city of London. This poem reflects my views on our welcomed friends who come from all parts of the world to start a new life in our country but there is a small element who would like to impose a more sinister side of their culture on the UK.

The British bulldog is
A friendly breed,
Tolerant and docile,
But looks and size
Do often deceive.

Don't push this dog
Against a wall.
His bite is terrible.
A horrific grip
Will bite off your fingers,
Chew them and spit.

Enjoy your freedom
In OUR pleasant land.
Your customs and culture
We understand

But don't force your will
Or alien ways
On a people and culture

That will NOT change.

We are British,
The bulldog breed.
Your terror and bombs
Will not succeed.

Throw the Dice

This is a true poem about a group of lads in New York who were caught gambling by the NYPD
    and brought before the judge for sentence. This is what one of them said:

Yes, your honour, I broke the law
By gambling with dice in a shop's front door

But you see, your honour,
I cannot read and these dice are Bibles to me.
These dice I hold within my hands
Do not make me an evil man.

A cube of wood or marble block
Marked on all sides with small black dots –
I beg you, sir, hear my plea of how these dice are a
Bible to me.

If I roll the dice and get the one,
That's God the father of everyone.

Roll again, up comes two,
I think of Jesus, who sacrificed for me and you.

Wisest kings in history,
You bet your life I rolled the three.

Throw the dice, it lands on four.
Matthew, Mark, Luke and John
are the four disciples with
These dots on.

Throw again, it lands on five.
I give praise to the Lord that I'm alive.

One more roll, it lands on six.
I remember that cross of sticks.

Jail me, fine me, if you will,
But let me keep my prayer block still.

The judge gave a slight smile and gave them six months
And said as he was passing sentence,

Tough luck, lads, I'm an atheist.

Tick-Tock

Tick-tock.

For every tick
Of that clock you hear
Heralds a death
Of a child who
Perished in fear.

Tick-tock.

Starving and gasping of
Unquenchable thirst,
The children of Africa
Are buried in earth.

Tick-tock.

This ticking won't stop,
But the peoples of earth
Can stop this death clock.

Tick-tock.

Make sure your money
Is spent on their need,
Not lining the pockets
Of unscrupulous greed.

Tick-tock.

Kick out the fat ones
Who cream from the top.
Make sure your money

Stops this tick-tock.

Time for a Change

In the UK we, the people, suffer the lowest form of crap that call themselves MPs. Every day we find that some cretin has been caught with their poxy finger in OUR cookie jar, hence this poem. We need someone to stick up for us and who is good at cutting fingers off.

The Labour Party, both old and new was due for the scrapyard long ago,

Their morals ditched like a ragged old coat. They take us ALL as a ruddy big joke.

They couldn't give a hoot for you and me, stuffing their faces into our money tree. Let's kick them out and start again, with a party in the workers' name.

We have the money, but do we have the balls to chuck out Labour, this middle-class crap, and elect our own pure left-winger fighting-class chaps?

Let's make the rules for the downtrodden ones, not for the rich and

Eton's sons but for pensioners and those on low pay, something that Labour did on far-off distant days.

Kick them out, every last one; they should kiss our feet and clean our bums for the massive damage they've done to us downtrodden ones.

Labour is tainted for ever more with greed and corruption. Spinning with lies, the nation don't trust them, just like that other blue crew who pinch our wealth that belongs to YOU.

So start a new party and make it quick. Drive a great wedge with a hammer and pick to stake OUR claim on this country of ours for the majority of workers in OUR country's name.

These times are dangerous for 'they' have much to lose, a lifestyle of luxuries with toadies afoot who will use all means for the status quo to bury you deep in the mire of deceit.

Start it now or forever regret when the BMP becomes a Parliamentary threat. We will be out in the cold, there on our own, for Labour and Tory and the Liberal lot will never defend us from this bigoted lot.

The blame for this will rest with you, the leaders of our unions,
    The keepers of our cash. Forget Labour and its corrupt and lying ways.
    Start OUR own party. Whatever it's called, let it be the lynchpin of power that works for all.

Time to Do or Die

It's time the working poor
Rose up to remove the chains
Of oppression fascist MPs have
locked on you. It's time
We threw out these Nazi bastards
Who despise and look down on you.

We are back in the days
Of Nazi Adolf Hitler who hated
The poor and underclass who
Ended up in gas chambers,
Just as the Jews of days gone past.

Gone are the safety nets that kept
The worst at bay, stolen are the
Allowances that kept starvation
Away. This fascist scum from Eton
Who could not give a shit if you froze
Or starved to death, but kept his kind
From it.

Fascist scum like Cameron
And the yellow bastard Clegg
Who sit there on their arseholes
Whilst poor are slowly bled.

It's time to do or die. We have
Nothing more to fucking lose.
Ransack this poxed-up Parliament

And bring these bastards down.
Throw the fascist in the sewer
And let the bastards drown.

Time for another poll tax time
When riots brought the Maggot
Down. Time for us to do or die

And rid the country of this vermin
To cease our children's hunger cries.
Time for all of us to raise the banner
Of freedom, so very, very high.

Tiny Hands

'Tis the whisper
Of a gurgling child,
The sounds of love
When he sees his mum
Or dad. His tiny son –

Little toes
And tiny feet,
A little mouth
Of velvet skin.
The baby smells
So small, so neat.

Tiny hands,
All fingers
And thumbs,
Holding on
To Dad's
And Mum's.

To

To give and not always take.
To love and never hate.
To look and not to see
All the injustice
Around you
And me.

Too Late for Tears

As her starving child lay dying in her
skeleton-like arms,
Her tiny child whispered to her African mother,
'Please, Mummy, is there nothing to eat?'
Looking at the vast arid wilderness all around
Her, she told this fairy tale to her dying child.

We have bayonet pudding
Or bullet pie.
We have half-track pancakes
And A-bomb fries.
There is gunship stew,
A toffee tank or two,
Bloodbath dips
With religious nuts
And cluster bombs
Like candy sticks,
Big fat pigs
You cannot eat.
They lined their pockets
With all your sweets –
Chocolate soldiers
Who rape and beat.

A grave she dug with bare hands
That covered her child in African sands.
A single tear is all she shed
As she nursed another one to her breast.

Tory Blair

Your lies and cheating are at an end.
Your cheating ways you can't defend.
Your pile of loot that made some rich.
Your promise to pensioners you swiftly
Ditched.

Your illegal criminal war in the Middle East.
Your subservience to Bush, the evil beast.
You've had it all and made a mess.
Your time is up, so clear your desk.

Your pension awaits you to spend
Your three million pounds, a PM's perk,
Your golden handshake.

You truly earned
Your Judas gold, your golden fleece.
Your tombstone reads, 'He destroyed
The peace.

Tory Boy

Well, the Tory toff has spilt the beans,
Saying the poor and fatties raise no sympathy.
You get short change with no help from me.

Well, you Eton-educated bum, David Cameron
To us humble ones, you make us sick with your
Stuck-up ways, downing the fat and underclass
Your ancestors may have been in years gone past.

You haven't a clue about how we 'others' live,
Tory boy,
With your kiss-curl quiff, as you have your lunch in
White's, your club. We make do with beans on toast
As you tuck in to your pheasant roast,

With your silver spoon stuck up your bum. How dare
You criticise the poor and fat ones? Your daddy gave
You all you've got, Tory boy, you spineless twat.
You're in good company with your Tory chums,
The Maggot and Tebbit to name but two.
The Hall of Shame is waiting for YOU.

On your bike, Tory boy.

Trust Betrayed

Never trust a byte in cyberspace
Or trust a human, whatever their race.
Trust betrayed, a deadliest of deeds,
So easy for some who lie and deceive.

Users and abusers they turn out to be
Who take the piss with impunity.
Words are cheap to this lowest of scum,
So beware, stay clear of this deadly one.
Knives in the back like Caesar of old –
Brutus and friends, my cyber chums.

U2 Brutus?

'Twas the Third of Never

'Twas a day so long ago
When spacemen first appeared,
A blazing ball of wind and fire
As they circled the earth
Till the flames expired.

Their craft came down
In the deserts of the east
As tall as a mountain,
A gleaming beast...

'God,' they cried,
In a cringing mass
At this mountain of technology
These earthlings did face,
Paying homage
To this celestial craft...

That stirred and hummed
With ear-splitting sounds
As creatures from space
Took stock of the humans
That had gathered around...

Then blazing lights in
Pencil-thin beams
Paralysed twelve earthlings
In a stone-like trance
As the creatures from space
Began to chant and dance...

We are from a distant star
Beyond your sun so very far.
This message we give
To these twelve men –
Mend your ways and live in peace
Or on the third of never
This Earth will cease...

We leave you now
But will be back in time
To see if our words
Have changed mankind...

You must be joking.

Twisted Oak

As I sit here quietly
Beneath your brow,
Your trunk all twisted
As you reach for the sky.
Your foliage and acorns,
The shade that you give
To this old man now
From when he was a kid...

In your magnificent age
I wonder and ponder
All you have seen
Over four hundred years
Of us human beings.

This twisted oak,
Over one hundred feet high,
Struck by lightning
Time after time

But even this force
Couldn't bring you down,
Only the chainsaw
Of the council clowns.

Two Cents a Bullet

Two cents a bullet, that's what it costs to die,
When soldiers wear their uniform to
defend the likes of
You and me.

Two cents of humanity of blood that's soaked in earth.
Two cents of glory, that how much a soldier's worth.

A body bag of blood and guts
and a flag that never flies,
That's draped upon a coffin then
folded in a pad and given
To his widow for that life he never had.

So two cents a bullet that all you're really worth.
Load them in your rifles, chums, and aim them at
The scum who made the bullets first.

Then pull the trigger firmly and spill
their blood on the earth.

Peter Wicks – a veteran of Cyprus and Egypt.
NS days (1955/57).

Valhalla

Odin's palace, the fortress of the slain,
and the land of gods, the kingdom of
Asgard, the Valkyries, these goddesses did name.

For those who died in battle were carried on
Golden shields held so very high
To a palace in the heavens, Valhalla in the sky.

Made of many weapons that adorned this mystic place,
Walls of spears and roofs of mirrored
Shields that reflected the warrior's face.

Fearsome warriors who pillaged old England's shores
Did battle with a brand of man whose
courage was never
Shamed – the Berserkers was their name.

Drinking jars of mead, these Norsemen
fought and died,
Then were carried to old Odin in his palace in the sky
Who made them well with a Valkyrie
spell to add his shield
To that magic roof some Christians would call hell.

Vets of Greed

Years ago, a veterinary surgeon would care for sick animals of those poor and needy in our society and their services were sometimes given for free or for whatever the pet owner could afford but today the poor find it hard and impossible to keep a pet in good health because the of the astronomical fees ALL vets charge, regardless if your pet is suffering great pain and discomfort. Caring for sick animals is a multibillion pound/dollar business for vets and insurance firms.

Don't have a pet if you are poor.
Never venture to a vet's front door.
Caring little if your pet's in pain,
But only for the fee you'll pay,
'Have you insurance?' they will ask.
So if you haven't, you can kiss their arse.
Caring and compassion has gone astray
For without insurance, you can't pay.
A creeping cancer of us human ones
When money and wealth
Always comes first
Before dumb animals' health.

Wake Up

Just had to make this point about the lot we elected to Westminster. To me they are a complete waste of space. None of them gives a toss about us, that is if you're not filthy rich and can afford to buy a knighthood. This poem is about the new buzz word for lying, these crooks call it spin; I call it a porky-pie.

Speaking with forked and lying tongues,
Never the simple truth to anyone,
Don't believe a word they ever say,
Spinning their lies to their heart's desire
As you murmur, 'You ruddy great liar.'

Spinning their lies on this and that,
Hoping the gullible will swallow their crap.
Like a dervish they spin around,
Spinning so fast they leave the ground.

An evil web is what they spin,
Lying and cheating on everything.
The polecats who we choose to rule
From all political colours and hues.

These toe-rags from the political class,
Not one of them are fit to kiss our arse.
Hateful, deceitful women and men.
Wake up, Great Britain.
Get rid of them.

Was It Worth It?

Was it worth the long river of young blood
Soldiers gave their countries that they loved?
Did they die for nothing, just pawns in a rich
Man's game, making endless profit from the
Armaments that fill their graves?

When did you see a senator or a British MP
Serving as a soldier or doing battle in Iraq,
Or the evil home of Afghanistan's bloody soil?
Never is the answer! Never for ever more.

Talk is cheap to these rich creeps and your life
Is worth not much, so tally-ho, off you go and fight
Our noble wars. Win or lose, they don't give a damn.
Ten million bullets at ten cents a time is a gold mine
In their hand.

So count the shrouds that cover our dead and ask
What was achieved. Someone made a fortune and
Our dead were terribly deceived by nasty political
Butchers and dirty bastard thieves.

We Are YOUR Masters (We Want It Back)

We, the people, reaffirm these facts,
Public servants of whatever your hue,
Do OUR bidding and not what suits you.

You are our servants, not the other way round.
You kiss our shoes and grovel on the stinking ground.
You eat the dirt that WE dish out so don't complain or
WE will kick you out.

We think you servants are overpaid,
especially those on centre stage.
WE never told you to help yourself to money
WE own by rates and rents that you
collect by force and threats.

We want control of what is OURS.
It never belonged to you, insipid shower.
WE want the rules that favour US and not the servants
WE no longer trust.

WE are YOUR masters. WE pull the strings.
WE will tell you when to dance and when to sing.
WE will set your wages and any other perks
WE are about to retrieve from you disgraceful jerks.

For WE have had enough of servants
who screw the very last drop

Of blood from the people who OWN you. Do as
WE say from this day on or take a long walk
On a very short plank and drown in the blood you
bastards have drunk.

So remember your place. WE are your bosses.
Servants must please the ones who pay
them and keep them
In check for, by the god Uranus, you'll
be out on your necks.

Do not move without OUR orders.
Jump and bow, fawn and cower to us, YOUR bosses,
You public servant shower.

We Plough the Fields

They blame it on the poorest ones
And force them all to pay the bill
For seeds of greed they scattered
In England's sacred lands
The poorest ones do till.

All the greed that surrounds us
Comes from crooks and thieves
Who sit there in governments.
Shamelessly they plot and plunder,
With cheating words to deceive.

You can blame it on the bankers,
The scumbags called City crooks,
Political lowlifes we elected to govern us –
The festering, leeching human pus
Who cooked the nation's books.

They gave out worthless mortgages
That were made of sick and snot,
The whole world brought in bundles,
Bankrupting the fucking lot.

They blame it on the poorest ones
And force them all to pay the bill
For seeds of greed they scattered
In England's sacred lands
The poorest ones do till.

Well Done, Saint Tony

You've made this world an unsafe place
for everyone in the human race.

You've got Bin Laden on the run,
Now he's after everyone.

You've walked on water, a saintly sight,
Pity your hands are blood-red bright.

You've talked to God or God to you.
Sorry, Tony, which one is true?

You've sent whitewash shares flying high.
Pity David Kelly had to die.

You've protected pensioners from Mr Brown.
Sorry, Tony, you let them down.

You've smiled and waved your saintly hands
Then sent our troops to desert sands.

You've declared a war that no one wants –
Just you and Bush and the petrol pumps.

Sorry, Tony, you've got to go. The nation is sick of this
One-man show.

Well, Is That It?

They stole our billions
That made them fat.
Does the whole world
Let them get away with that?

We lost our house,
Our place of rest.
They made a fortune
From this ruddy mess.
When will justice
Take its cause
To haul these cretins
Before the courts?

If we steal or break the law
They send us to jail
For ever more.
But thieving bankers,
Wall Street thieves,
Committed theft
Beyond belief.

'Bail them out,'
Politicians cry,
But care nothing
For you or me.
Well, is that it?

Do these bandits
Get away with it?
Trust in banks

Has gone for good.
Come back my friend
Called Robin Hood.

What Has Happened in the
Land of the Free?

Where is free speech in the land of the free?
What has happened to YOUR DEMOCRACY?
Why are you scared to shout and protest?
Where is the America we love the best?

Who are the freaks who make up your rules,
Taping up your mouths to keep you in check,
The beginning of oppression by fascist fools?

Cut off the chains that bind you so tight
To bigots and crooks and government tripe and
Threaten your freedoms, your own way of life,
To jail you and kill you if you cause civil strife.

Rise up you people in the land of the free.
Don't let dictators threaten democracy.
Tear up the laws that bind you in chains.
Point at the scum who you must blame.

Take back the media that pumps out its hate.
Take back America before it's far too late.

What Have We Become?

A sense of foreboding hangs over me.
Isolation, depravation, dehumanisation,

Uncaring and selfishness is all that I see
As crowds of people, rush on by
Caring or thinking nothing for you or me.

Wrapped up in snug little insular worlds,
Society is crumbling but not a soul is disturbed.
The rich get richer on the backs of the poor
As the underclass grows bigger, a festering sore.

Immigrants flood in, wave after wave.
Governments care little for the disasters in store
As a meltdown of our nation threatens our shores.

Cohesion of the family, the bedrock of life
Is coming apart, as religion creates hatred in our midst
And splits up our proud nation and casts it adrift.

What is Reality?

Some time ago I wrote a poem on reality, not in my usual format, but as a list of 'reality sayings' that have come my way as I walked down life's highway. This is my up-dated list:

Reality is knowing that night will follow day and that
Justice is for those who can afford it.

Reality is that we sit on a seat of high-born morality
And opulence, preaching our corrupt ways to
those who
Languish and die in poverty and starvation.

Reality is knowing that that bluebottle flies buzzing
Around your body as you take your last breath will be
Alive when you are dead.

Reality is – the meek will NOT inherit the earth. The
Strong will see to that.

Reality is knowing that you married for MONEY and
you
Spend most of your life looking for LOVE.

Reality is knowing the difference between an
intellectual
Snob and a monetary snob. The latter is easy to spot –
Just look at the wallet.

Reality is knowing that talk is cheap and that action
Speaks louder than words BUT talk don't cost a penny.

Reality is knowing when to let go OR risk going down
With them.

Reality is when you marry OUT of your class.
This can be
A disaster as you spend the rest of your life trying to
Be someone you're not.

Reality is that communications are instant but food aid
Is not as fast.

Reality is that the WHOLE world
knows the war in Iraq is
Unwinnable. Could someone remove the rose-coloured
Glasses from Bush and Blair?

Reality is that some live high on the hog. The rest
Live on the scraps thrown to them.s

What Was It All About?

Born into poverty as the third of a tribe of five
Who struggled with great adversity just to stay alive,

Wickedness I have seen, most directed at me,
By a mother full of hate for the third one in her family.

But that was many years ago and time
just marches on and
New scars will take their place
On a life spent on giving to the only child I ever had,
Who only takes with grasping hands.

Brainwashed by his evil mate who takes but never gives
Our love for them and all their kids that
we gave them on a plate.

For a son is a son till he takes a wife,
thereafter she dictates
The direction of his life –

To cast his mum and dad adrift and fleece
them of their wealth,
Then put them in a dustbin that robs
them of their health.

So the wheel of life has gone around for
this lad of long ago,
Who tried and lost the battle we would
never win with the whore
Of a woman who is my son's wife.

When the Bubble Burst

This fool's paradise had to end.
Your bricks and mortar
Are not worth a trite
As houses prices collapsed
One dark, bleak winter's night.

Great big debt around your necks –
Seizing your home, your worldly goods,
Your lifestyle is now an utter wreck.

Big burly bailiff knocks down your door,
Taking your car and all your worldly goods,
Kicking you out into your neighbourhood.

Penniless and homeless, and you had it all.
As the bubble bursts on greedy young fools,
You're not alone. We have seen this before
When house prices crashed down to the floor.

No one listened to those wise ones of old
Who warned of this disaster about to unfold.
Bricks and mortar or just a fleeting fortune
For he who pays the piper also calls the tune.
They want their money back.
It never belonged to you.

Where Have All the Gardens Gone?

Office blocks that are forever empty
Rise to the heavens to the gods of plenty.
This land they stand on should rather be
A place of beauty, with parks and trees.

This concrete jungle, stone-grey streets
Which breed contempt and a violent streak.
For the youth today have no home,
Forever trapped by cement, brick and stone.

The money gods of Hampstead Heath
Could do lots more for the young ones' grief.
Take the Bishops Avenue and Willesden Green,
They are as different as chalk and cheese.

Ten-room homes with swimming pools,
Tennis courts and croquet lawns,
Just a mile away, just down the road –
Bitterness and contempt slowly grows.

In one-room flats in dingy streets
The youth of London live and sleep, with
Outside loos and roofs that leak.

They do their best to pay their rent
To crooked landlords who collect and threaten
For it's in this city of dirt and grime
Some London youth will turn to crime.

They know full well they have no choice
Against the might of a bureaucrat's voice.

The money gods and their might
Could do lots more for the young ones' plight.
Instead of building these high-rise blocks
Of monstrous offices and empty shops,
Invest their wealth in open spaces,
Low-level houses with gardens to grace
For if this dream could come true
The kids of London could be like me or you.

Who Are we?

We are obsessed by who we are,
Our lineage and the family tree.
Who is who? Does it belong to me?
Class and standing within your rank are
Judged by where we come from,
Not the vast fortunes in the bank.

We British are a snooty, snobby lot.
The whole world knows this is true.
Breeding is important at the very top.
It classifies us in status,
The personage of you.

The working class,
They know their place –
The bottom of the heap,
Manual jobs and fighting wars.
This status this lot do keep.

The middle class,
The yuppies of yesterday,
They own the business
That pays the cash
To working-class lads and lasses.

The upper class,
The establishment elite,
They own it all, the ruddy lot.
This breeding is quite unique –
A silver spoon stuck up their arse
With shit for brains they do speak.

Who Cares?

Who gives a toss
About the carers' lot?
The six million
This New Labour
Conveniently forgot.

They care for us
Both night and day.
Some don't get
A penny in basic pay
As they care for others
Twenty-four hours a day.

Ebenezer Scrooge
Would rub his hands
At the restrictions
Conjured up
By Labour creeps
That deny carers
The very basics.

A labour of love,
Some would say,
But respite care
With a little pay
Would help
In this 24/7
Endless day.

Who Do They Think They Are?

Who are these creatures who preach to you?
What right do they have to tell us what to do?

Do they come from Earth or from some unknown star
Which has superior intellect and an
authoritarian persona that
Shines above their head just like a halo
of the angel of death?

What right do they have to force unjust laws down our
Throats that cripple a nation till we nearly all choke?
Who gave them the power to do as they please and
bankrupt the world?

These bankers who thieve – who gave the City,
and Wall Street as well,
The right to gamble with money that
came from the poor that pushed
The whole system down into recession once more?

Did you tell them they could do it to
make the elite rich? To bend
Any rule and use any tricks to make you
all homeless and strip
You of wealth and spit in your face
and take all your jobs?
Then take them to China to be done
on the cheap for five yuan a
Week and hovels they keep.

How come you're dying for want
of health care and the
Bastards who have it just look
at you and stare and demand a
King's ransom for a lump of band-aid
tape to stop a child's
Bleeding or to save someone's life.

If your insurance has ended and
you can't pay the bill to
Arseholes of doctors who live off the
cream that the vilest of the
Vile pharmaceuticals gives them
that makes them stinking rich
And the Hippocratic Oath these
bastards all ditched...

So, who can get justice that cost
your arm or a leg from a
Crooked attorney who just wants your bucks?
And when you
Land up in jail doesn't give a blind fuck.

Just pay up your cash and he
will see what's to do.
Bribe all the judges for they are crooks too.

What is there left in the land of the
free when all of your jobs
Are in JAP industry and they sold them
to China for a mountain of debt
that all of you Americans have got to pay yet?

So let's recap at all we have seen.
Was this the meaning of the
Republicans' dream? Of Bush and his
cohorts, his advisers in
Black, to sell off America and all it
holds dear, to Chinese in Asia
With two billion or more peasants as
workers that will make US ALL POOR?

Who Gives a Donald Duck?

Who gives Donald about the war dead?
Does Bush or Blair or even Brown
Give a tom-tit if the whole of
Iraq just drowns?

Blood and guts mean nothing to this lot.
Ten cents a bullet – let them die,
Just as easy as swatting flies.

Who gives a Donald about our lads,
The ones some kids call their dads?
And who gives a tommy-tit that
Their dads are maimed or blown to bits?
Not many I fear could give a damn
About our lads in far-off lands.

Pass a law and make it fast
That all the MPs who vote for war
Are the first ones sent to foreign shores.
Let them fight with senators from the States and
Be first to die for their blundering mistakes.

The truth would be that there is
not the slightest doubt
They would run and run if someone
fired a starting gun.
Wars would be a distant dream if MPs and senators
Were the first to be drafted to a conflict scene.

Rectum wobble or bubbling bum
would be all you'd see
From these elitist ones but there again, they would
Float to the top, like turds in cauldron
when it got too hot.

Who Gives a Toss?

This is Britain, 2010. Do the old and frail
Of Britain feel safe in this uncaring violent place?

In modern Britain, the old and frail, the weak and sick
Are preyed on by unscrupulous greedy youngsters
By chance they meet.

Even their children, who couldn't care less in a society
Full of unbridled greed, take and swindle and often
Thieve their parents' money, their pension pot, taking
It all, the whole ruddy lot.

Gone are the days of caring for mum for most of the
Daughters are lower than scum, as are
sons their parents
Never see who father grandchildren by different
Mums. Just like their sisters they're lower than scum.

So gone forever the old-fashioned ways, when dads
And mums held sway over all. Now greedy kids take
And they steal, before the ink is dry on their wills.

A portrait of Britain, 2014.

Who Knows?

Who knows if you will live or die?
The choice does not belong to you or me.

'Count to ten,' the anaesthetist said.
But you remember nothing; you could be dead.

Then you wake from that cold dark sleep
With tubes and bags from your head to your feet.

Water flows in a constant drip,
Saline solution flowing through
A tube into your dick into your bladder.
The fluid floods to wash out the cancer
That's mixed with your blood.

Then it's the chemo,
Not a treatment of choice,
That pulls out your hair
In massive great lumps
And the sickness is awful
That keeps you down in the dumps.
Then your eyebrows fall out
And your eyelashes too.
The baldness is complete
For this is the new you.

Now the whispers of hair
Are back on my head
And I'm glad that I made it
And I'm back from the dead.

But cancer is terrible
Which you must really fight
Or give up the ghost
And die in your bed
In the darkness of night.

Why War

Most modern wars are fought for gold!
Black Gold, or Texas tea.
Just plain old oil, to you or me.

This sticky mess that fuels our cars
Sends countless thousands to the knacker's yard.
They want the oil from desert sands
Far away from their corrupted land.

They want a pipeline from East to West
Through Baltic lands or Arab States –
And create a war, if all this takes.

They need this oil to feed their greed,
To bolster their wealth, with us in need,
The sickest souls in humanity,

Who slaughter their own for Texas tea.
Not one of THEM would send their sons
To fight the wars that THEY've begun.

Kick out these devils before it's too late
Or the hands of Satan will rattle your gate.

Within My Mind

To have the power
For just one day
To banish mankind's
Evil far away.

To cure the sick,
The demented mind
Erased for ever
Till the ends of time.

With just one look
And claps of thunder
I would wave my hands
To wipe out hunger.

The pains of man,
His demented soul,
The need for greed,
His love of gold –

To give him wisdom,
The eyes to see
To change his ways
For all humanity.

He must understand
This is just a dream
But he must do his best
To make this a reality.

This I know beyond a doubt:
We will perish as a species
As the dodo has done
If we don't respect this Earth
As nature's true sons.

Woman In the Woods

When I was a young lad
And at my mother's side,
I wandered through a local wood
One sunny autumn day.

I met a woman standing there,
Her hair was golden bright.
She smiled at me and cast a spell
Beneath that autumn light.

Come look into my blue eyes
And at my golden hair.
Remember this, throughout your life,
You will never meet a woman
Who is quite so fair.

She told me many stories
Of life and love's delights
But now I am an old man
Who has nearly reached his time.

But I remember vividly
That day in the woods and
The tales and stories told to me
By the woman in the woods.

Woodvine Cottage

Sleeping deep
In woods and vales
Far from tracks
And hiking trails.

Broad oak trees
In woodland shade,
Flickering sunlight
On beasts who graze.

Pastures green
By a meandering stream,
The music of skylarks
High on the wing.

A tranquil white cottage
Appears on the scene.
Hollyhocks and ivy
Cling to the walls
Of this tiny white cottage
So sweet and serene.

'Woodvine Cottage'
The nameplate says,
As you open the gate
Onto a twisting pathway.
Borders of flowers
All colours and hues
Add to the beauty
With a heady perfume.

'Good morning, my dear,'
The young woman says,
As she opens the door
Of the house of my dreams.

My dream is broken.
The dream is no more.
I wake from my sleep
Untroubled or stressed.
This cottage is mine
My home and my rest.

You Can't Take It With You

All that wealth, your worldly goods,
Fabulous fortunes, the stuff of gods
You lied and cheated to make this so,
But YOU can't take it with you
On that journey we ALL undergo.

Now make amends
For the deeds you've done,
Ebenezer Scrooge, you miserly one.

Give your money, all your goods
To all those children with nought at all.
Smiles of pleasure is a gift, you fools.

Spend it NOW, don't let it rot
Or as sure as night follows day
The taxman will grab the LOT.

You've Blown It, Labour

You took a massive beating in 2010
And it looks like it will happen again.
You've lost the plot, you stupid twats,
Enclosed in your bubble, a fairy's nest,
The unreal world of technocrats.

It was Tory Blair who destroyed our faith
In all things socialist that we once embraced,
Plus Brown and Mandelson, lying cow sons,
Like Machiavellian wizards created the hated PFI
That sold the welfare state belonging to you and me.

Hoodwinking our unions with 'jam tomorrow',
They ploughed in millions for lies so hollow.
Union leaders gave pots of OUR money away
So ermine robes would grace their backs
As in the House of Lords they finally sat.

You've blown it, Labour, with the working class
As you talk and babble of the upper-middle ones.
We are told to bend down and kiss their arse.
Labour is stone-like dead and must be revived.
The Miliband millionaires in front-row seats
Will lead OUR party into certain defeat.
A working-class hero is what OUR party needs –
REAL working socialists for the party to succeed.

Old-fashioned socialists and not multimillionaires
Must take over Labour for the working class,

Just as they did in Nye Bevan's days
When nationalisation of everything
Gave us workers the socialist dream.

So pack your bags, you must go
For we are sick and tired
Of Ed Miliband's one-man show.

You've blown it, Ed. Now just piss off
And go.